Herbert Hoover at the Onset of the Great Depression, 1929-1930

Robert Sobel

New College of Hofstra

The America's Alternatives Series

Edited by **Harold M. Hyman**

Herbert Hoover

at the Onset of the Great Depression, 1929-1930

J. B. Lippincott Company
Philadelphia/New York/Toronto

ISBN 0-397-47334-6
Library of Congress Catalog Card Number 74-23096
Printed in the United States of America

1 3 5 7 9 8 6 4 2

Library of Congress Cataloging in Publication Data

Sobel, Robert.
    Herbert Hoover at the onset of the great depression
1929-1930

    (The America's alternatives series)
    Bibliography: p.
    1. United States—Politics and government—1929-19
2. Hoover, Herbert Clark, Pres. U.S., 1874-1964.
3. Depressions—1929—United States. I. Title.
E801.S65   973.91'6'0924   74-23096
ISBN 0-397-47334-6

Contents ═══════════════════

Foreword

"When you judge decisions, you have to judge them in the light of what there was available to do it," noted Secretary of State George C. Marshall to the Senate Committees on the Armed Services and Foreign Relations in May 1951.[1] In this spirit, each volume in the "America's Alternatives" series examines the past for insights which History—perhaps only History—is peculiarly fitted to offer. In each volume the author seeks to learn why decision-makers in crucial public policy or, more rarely, private choice situations adopted a course and rejected others. Within this context of choices, the author may ask what influence then-existing expert opinion, administrative structures, and budgetary factors exerted in shaping decisions? What weights did constitutions or traditions have? What did men hope for or fear? On what information did they base their decisions? Once a decision was made, how was the decision-maker able to enforce it? What attitudes prevailed toward nationality, race, region, religion, or sex, and how did these attitudes modify results?

We freely ask such questions of the events of our time. This "America's Alternatives" volume transfers appropriate versions of such queries to the past.

In examining those elements that were a part of a crucial historical decision, the author has refrained from making judgments based upon attitudes, information, or values that were not current at the time the decision was made. Instead, as much as possible he or she has explored the past in terms of data and prejudices known to persons contemporary to the event.

1. U.S. Senate, Hearings Before the Committees on the Armed Services and the Foreign Relations of the United States, *The Military Situation in the Far East* (82 Cong., 2d sess.), Part I, p. 382. Professor Ernest R. May's "Alternatives" volume directed me to this source and quotation.

Nevertheless, the following reconstruction of one of America's major alternative choices speaks implicitly and frequently, explicitly to present concerns.

In form, this volume consists of a narrative and analytical historical essay (Part One), within which the author has identified by use of headnotes (i.e., Alternative 1, etc.) the choices which he believes were actually before the decision-makers with whom he is concerned.

Part Two of this volume contains, in whole or part, the most appropriate source documents that illustrate the Part One Alternatives. The Part Two Documents and Part One essay are keyed for convenient use (i.e., references in Part One will direct readers to appropriate Part Two Documents). The volume's Part Three offers users further guidance in the form of a bibliographic essay.

Professor Robert Sobel reviews in this forceful and penetrating volume the public policy decisions centering on the effects of what was becoming the Great Depression, made and refused by President Herbert Hoover.

The analysis and documents presented by Professor Sobel take the reader through a time which was ripping away from what contemporaries thought was history's firm moorings, but which had not yet revealed the best road to a future. The treatment stresses continuities and complexities instead of the overly simple insistence by most commentators on sharp choice decisions.

Harold M. Hyman
Rice University

Preface

With the exception of the Civil War, the Great Depression of the 1930s left more scars on the American character than any other national experience. Clearly it is one of the major watersheds in our history. Perhaps it is to be expected that in the popular literature and much of the history written of this decade it is made to appear that Americans had one set of values prior to 1929, and another afterwards.

In this kind of analysis, Franklin D. Roosevelt is made to symbolize a new way of viewing government and political philosophy. For the past two generations, historians have generally sympathized with Roosevelt, and found him admirable. A reaction is setting in today, but it is doubtful that the general view of Roosevelt as the man who saved us from the depression will change much—at least among the general public.

Dramatists of history, needing a protagonist, have selected Herbert Hoover for the role, one which Hoover willingly and even eagerly accepted. He has become—again, in the popular view—the exemplar for the old way of life. Yet Hoover was no reactionary, but an able, activist, thoroughly modern leader, whose willingness to expand the powers of the presidency and even of government, and to use both to combat the depression, led some to consider him socialistic in 1929-1930.

Hoover was the spokesman for a philosophy of government, the associational movement, as important in its own way as progressivism before it and the New Deal afterwards. It is not as familiar to students as the New Freedom of Woodrow Wilson or the New Deal of Franklin Roosevelt, just as the term, "New Era," used as a rubric for the late 1920s, has fallen into disuse. Yet had the depression not taken place, the associational movement might still be popular today. Without the depression Hoover would have gone on to a second term and retired in triumph in 1937, after preparing for a successor with the same view of government as his. In such a scenario, the associational movement, not progressivism and certainly not the New Deal (for it would not have occurred without the depression), would have been viewed by many historians today as a proper twentieth-century response to the problems of modern industry and society.

But the depression did take place. Beginning in 1929, two presidents attempted to deal with it, both having little success. Adolph Hitler and World War II, not Herbert Hoover and the New Era or Franklin D. Roosevelt and the New Deal, brought the nation out of its economic doldrums.

Today historians see continuities between the New Era and the New Deal. Hoover rejected such a notion. He believed his administration was the last gasp of freedom in America, the last dedicated to capitalism and freedom, before the nation succumbed to socialism and alien ideology. In 1929-1930 he looked upon the depression as another decline in the business cycle, comparable to those the nation underwent in 1921, 1907, and 1893. Hoover did not realize the magnitude of the depression at the time, and for the rest of his life attempted to defend his position, stating that he not only understood the problem, but was responding to it in a way consistent with freedom and responsibility.

Yet very few people, and none of these in power, believed in 1929-1930 that what appeared to be a tidal wave was actually the first stage of a hurricane. By the end of the first year of the depression, some had come to realize that they were in the midst of a movement that almost defied understanding and solution. Perhaps, they thought, future generations would understand it better. "What a strange situation confronts us today," said Representative James Mead of New York.

> Will not our grandchildren regard it as quite incomprehensible that in 1930 millions of Americans went hungry because they had produced too much food; that millions of men, women, and children were cold because they produced too much clothing, that they suffered from the chilly blasts of winter because they produced too much coal? I am not speaking in parables, this is the literal truth. To-day we are suffering want in the midst of unprecedented plenty. Our workers are without wages because they have learned to work too well. . . .[1]

In the 1970s the grandchildren of the men in power at that time still debate the causes of the depression; of the many theories they offer in this regard, none are entirely satisfactory. Historians still argue as to the beginning date, although economists no longer find it incomprehensible that there can be want in the midst of plenty. But they still have not found a solution to this paradox that would be consistent with the kind of freedom Hoover spoke of in 1930. We have a better perspective on the problems today, and even a better understanding of them, but the solutions still evade us.

This book is an attempt to understand Hoover's actions in the context of his own times. To do this one must first appreciate the basic assumptions

---

1. Jordan A. Schwartz, *The Interregnum of Despair: Hoover, Congress, and the Depression* (Urbana; University of Illinois Press 1970), p. 31.

about man and society Hoover brought to office. These had developed over half a century from the crude Social Darwinism of the late nineteenth century to the associational philosophy of the 1920s. Hoover was a forceful spokesman for his point of view; more than most national leaders, he remained consistent in this throughout his life, even while his actions changed to meet the needs of different circumstances.

One must also appreciate the position Hoover held in the nation in the late 1920s. To many he was more than a president; he was part of their vision of the future, one in which freedom would be wedded with technology. Hoover appeared as a political leader, business genius, major intellectual, a scientist with few peers, and a secular saint to a generation that grew into maturity after what was then called the Great War and which we call World War I. He was, then, a combination of Washington, Thomas Edison, Andrew Carnegie, H.G. Wells, and St. Francis. Not since pre-Civil War days, or at least the time of U.S. Grant, had a man entered the White House with such a reputation. No man appeared so well qualified for the position as did Hoover in 1929.

Hoover would serve as president for half a year before the stock market crash of October, 1929 awakened most Americans to their economic difficulties. In this period—one many historians have neglected—he attempted to put his ideas into practice in a consistent fashion, and in the process earned a reputation as a forceful, strong president. He also recognized weaknesses in the economy, and prepared for a depression—one he thought would be "another 1921." When the depression came, he implemented these ideas, and in a vigorous fashion. Although Hoover did more in the emergency than had any of his predecessors during previous depressions, it was not enough. Like so many others, he was a casualty of that period of great misery, and in a matter of a few years was looked upon as a symbol of the failures of the "old ways."

During the next generation it would be fashionable to write of the shortsightedness of the Hoover administration, especially during that first year of the Great Depression. The president was usually castigated for his timidity and lack of sympathy for the starving, and considered inept in the face of great crisis. The man who had received over fifty-eight percent of the popular vote in 1929 won less than forty percent four years later, and went into eclipse. For the rest of his life he would defend his record, well into the 1960s, long after such matters held much interest for a majority of Americans. Hoover appeared antique and quaint by then, an almost laughable figure, like an old general attempting to apply the lessons of the Spanish-American War to World War I. In this respect, Hoover proved one of his own worst enemies, and in a way contributed to the legend of his failures.

A different case can be made for him by studying his activities, especially at the onset of the depression, in the light of the times. Hoover was no reactionary. Nor was he a believer in received truths. His was one of the very few major attempts to adapt late nineteenth-century American values, formed in an agrarian age, to the economic and social realities of the early twentieth century. He provided an alternative to the various progressive ideologies of the time—those of Theodore Roosevelt, Woodrow Wilson, and Robert LaFollette, among others—and the socialism of Eugene V. Debs and his followers. Like Wilson, Hoover saw in the Russian Revolution a threat to western civilization. He attempted to rally capitalism and reform it to meet the challenge, as he and millions of others in the 1920s saw it. Hoover would wed science to business, the ideology of Thomas Jefferson to the world of Radio Corporation of America and General Motors, while maintaining traditional American values. He applied these ideas during the depression, in the face of opponents who claimed he was overreacting. In the process, Hoover widened the powers of the presidency more than most chief executives. The Hoover response to the Great Depression was vigorous, even imaginative.

Hoover might have responded differently to the depression. Men of great reputation and acknowledged wisdom urged different courses of action upon him. Some of his leading advisors preferred a laissez faire approach. Any attempt on the part of government to interfere with the "natural order" was not only unwise and destructive of freedom, they said, but would be counterproductive. Others, usually found among Hoover's opponents, favored such conventional palliatives as tariff reform, currency manipulation, and other programs that had been raised, and usually rejected, during the pre-World War I reform period. There were some who suggested solutions based on Italian fascism, others upon Russian communism. But in that first year of the depression Hoover's major critics came from the political and social right, men who felt he was "going too far," and from congressional Democrats who, for a variety of reasons, criticized Hoover without offering much in the way of alternatives. These would come later, in the form of the New Deal. But at the onset of the depression, Rooseveltian measures referred to those employed by Teddy, not those developed later on by FDR.

Hoover retained his long-developing and by 1929 mature philosophy of associationalism. He applied its principles in 1929-1930, and considered them a success. His opponents thought otherwise. In the end, Hoover lost his battle. Associationalism as a major means of meeting the challenge of the twentieth century economy faltered and declined. Little is heard of it today. But to many Americans in the days of Herbert Hoover it seemed the best alternative.

Robert Sobel
Hofstra University

Acknowledgments ===

Friends and critics (some combined in the same person) contributed, directly and indirectly, to the formulation of ideas presented and discussed in this work. Conversations over the years with Myron Luke provided insights into the period which molded my own. I benefitted greatly from a pleasant afternoon's discussion with Robert F. Himmelberg, and am most grateful for the many suggestions he put forth to one whose work parallels his own. As always, Professor Harold Hyman has been a wise and sensitive editor.

Part One ════════

═══════ The
Associational
Movement
and Its
Alternatives

1

The Transformation of the Business Ideology

Americans have a penchant for placing labels on decades, as though these ten year spans were natural chapters in the nation's history. They celebrate the presumed differences between them by assigning moods and values to each. In the process, they distort and often falsely shape beliefs regarding the historical process.

In their desire to have cut-and-dried slices of the national past, Americans often label decades before they can be considered in the perspective of time. They are dubbed before they are even completed. So it was that in 1960 some Americans hailed the advent of the "Soaring Sixties," later viewed as the most divisive and troubled period in the nation's history since the Civil War. To those who lived through the 1950s, that decade seemed exciting and eventful. Now it is known as the "Silent Decade." The 1890s, a time of much misery and strife, was called the "Gay Nineties" later on, even by people who should have known better.

The 1920s has been given several titles, such as the "Roaring Twenties," the "Golden Twenties," the "Jazz Decade," and "Normalcy." For some it was the last happy period in the nation's history, marked by innocence and progress. Others saw it as a time of crime and disorder, of lost opportunities, the prelude to disaster.[1]

Such thinking is not only confused and confusing, but it exaggerates, oversimplifies, and deceives. Apart from the obvious fact that the artificial water shed of New Year's Day of a year ending in zero is not a satisfactory demarcation point, elements of continuity in all these cases were more important than those of discontinuity. An understanding of the 1920s, for example, may be derived in part from the consideration of such factors as the growth of urbanization and the development of new technologies, the nature of economic growth, and the development of new forms of communication and transportation. At the same time, it should be recognized that all of these factors had roots in pre-World War I America, and some went back into the nineteenth century.

The "Received Truths" of the Twenties

A man or woman thirty years old in 1920 had been born in 1890. He or she had grown up in preautomobile and preradio times, and like most native-born Americans, had been raised in a small town or on a farm. The nation considered itself insulated from foreign problems by two major oceans. Even government was not considered a major force in the national life; the local justice of the peace and mayor had greater impacts on most people's day-to-day existence than the president.

President Benjamin Harrison knew this, and acted accordingly. Harrison lived a leisurely life by the standards of today. He rarely worked in the afternoons, for example, devoting that time of day to strolls or billiards. Harrison retired at nine o'clock most evenings, soon after dinner, and would sleep until six o'clock the next morning. He could take long vacations, and spend the better part of three days deciding whether or not to install electricity in the White House, having no other major problem to consider at the time. Grover Cleveland, who both preceded and followed Harrison in the White House, would say, in a moment of national crisis, that it was the business of the people to support the government, but that the government had no obligation to support the people. Future generations would consider this a strange statement, but at the time it was a reflection of the conventional wisdom.

The attitudes and fundamental beliefs of the thirty-year-old of 1920, formed before the turn of the century, were superimposed upon and confronted by a different kind of world. The Indiana farmboy of 1898, to whom a Pullman trip to Chicago seemed great adventure, marvelled in 1927 at Charles Lindburgh's solo flight across the Atlantic in an airplane—which had been developed after his birth. The New York woman of 1925, who as a child had considered recreation as consisting of church socials and family gatherings, now went to the movies, owned a radio, and considered the purchase of an automobile. The young man of 1905, to whom a high school diploma had seemed a sign of intellectual prowess, now functioned in a world where colleges were opening to the middle class, if not yet to the poor, while work, once the reason for man's existence on earth, was now deemed only a part of a person's life, undertaken primarily to enjoy pleasures of recreation and leisure afterwards.

Technological advancements, the dislocations caused by the world war, and the urbanization of the nation had caused one of the greatest transformations of American life since the nation's founding. Most were able to make the adjustment. But in so doing, they managed to bring the attitudes and values of the 1890s to the world of the 1920s. At times it seemed a strange fit.

Consider the case of a middle-aged woman who lived in Muncie, Indiana, the wife of a pipe-fitter, mother of two teen-aged boys. Her own mother had been a housewife; she went outside the home to do cleaning work six days a week. In so doing, she appeared a "liberated woman." But her views toward work, regarding accomplishment, her symbols of success, were as much a part of the age of Horatio Alger as that of F. Scott Fitzgerald, and contained elements of both.

> I began to work during the war, when every one else did; we had to meet payments on our house and everything else was getting so high. The mister objected at first, but now he don't mind. I'd rather keep on working so my boys can play football and basketball and have spending money their father can't give them. We've built our own home, a nice brown and white bungalow, by a building and loan like every one else does. We have it almost all paid off and it's worth about $6,000. No, I don't lose out with my neighbors because I work; some of them have jobs and those who don't envy us who do. I have felt better since I worked than ever before in my life. I get up at five-thirty. My husband takes his dinner and the boys buy theirs uptown and I cook supper. We have an electric washing machine, electric iron, and vacuum sweeper. I don't even have to ask my husband any more because I buy these things with my own money. I bought an icebox last year—a big one that holds 125 pounds; most of the time I don't fill it, but we have our folks visit us from back East and then I do. We own a $1,200 Studebaker with a nice California top, semi-enclosed. Last summer we all spent our vacation going back to Pennsylvania—taking in Niagara Falls on the way. The two boys want to go to college, and I want them to. I graduated from high school myself, but feel if I can't give my boys a little more all my work will have been useless.[2]

Such a woman probably knew veterans of the Civil War—there were 244,000 of them still alive in 1920. Civil War veterans were in Congress, and a hero of that conflict, Oliver Wendell Holmes, sat on the Supreme Court. Theodore Roosevelt, who died in 1919, was born in 1858, when James Buchanan was in the White House; William Howard Taft and Woodrow Wilson were also antebellum babies. Warren Harding, whose presidency began in 1921, was born in 1865, the year the Civil War ended. Calvin Coolidge, born on Independence Day, 1872, was elected to his first public office in 1899. Herbert Hoover, born in 1874, worked in western mines at a time when the Indian Wars were still on.

With the exception of Taft, who grew up in Cincinnati, Ohio, all of these men were raised in rural or semirural settings. The men who held power in America in the 1920s were too old to have fought in World War I, for the most part were insufficiently interested to volunteer for the Spanish-American War, but had close relatives with memories of the Civil War.

The Business Ideology

Secretary of the Treasury Andrew Mellon, one of America's wealthiest men, of whom it was said that "three presidents served under him," was born in 1855, and remembered Lincoln's assassination. He had met men and women whose fathers had served in the American Revolution, who had known Washington. Mellon may not have been as popular or glamorous as Charles Lindbergh, but he had more power than the aviator. His view of history—of his own past in particular—would determine his reactions to events of the 1920s—of which Lindbergh seems now a more fitting symbol.

A boy during the Civil War, an adolescent during Reconstruction, Mellon went into the lumber and building business in 1872, and two years later joined his father's bank in Pittsburgh. In the last quarter of the nineteenth century he was a leader in regional banking, a founder of the Aluminum Company of America, a man who had parried with the Rockefellers and won, and the holder of directorship in dozens of corporations. In the first decade of the new century he helped found Gulf Oil, and the Mellons had major interests in iron, steel, and coke. By then the family's assets placed it among the nation's wealthiest. On the eve of the first world war, the Mellons were said to be worth in the neighborhood of a billion dollars.

Mellon was Secretary of Treasury in the 1920s, when he was called "the greatest secretary of the treasury since Alexander Hamilton." But he maintained the business ideology throughout his life. As one of the so-called robber barons, he had been castigated for his actions at the turn of the century and the years that followed. Men like Theodore Roosevelt, Robert LaFollette and Woodrow Wilson had considered him and his kind as "malefactors of great wealth," and had called for their destruction (although their rhetoric was exaggerated). Mellon had survived such verbal assaults, though he was irritated by them, and resented the reputation of exploiter, when he considered himself a benefactor. Now he was in the cabinet. Business not only was respectable, but businessmen respected. In the 1920s, men who admired Andrew Mellon would attempt to graft the business ideology of the late nineteenth century onto the social structure of the third decade of the twentieth century. They would take the "given" truths of their youth, and try to superimpose them upon the quite different technological and social structure of Lindbergh's America. As with the Muncie housewife, the fit would be uneven.

The old ideology was both simple and appealing. It was rooted in the Puritan ethic, which among other things held that the "Elect" would justify themselves through their public activities. Adam Smith provided the ideology with economic justifications in his *Wealth of Nations* (1776) and demonstrated that all segments of society benefitted when the government maintained a hands-off policy. Those who survived in such an atmosphere were, by implication, also of the Elect. The Social Darwinists reinforced the Puritans and liberal economists when they observed that "the survival of the fittest" obtained in business as well as in biology, and to interfere with competition would cause grave damage to the nation's social and moral fabric. American businessmen applauded English philosopher Herbert Spencer, whose writings on the subject were popular in their circles, but they were Social Darwinists before the term had been coined. The ideology provided a rationale for developments that already had taken place, were in the process of developing, or that were planned by the industrialists and bankers to suit their own ends.

In a land blessed with plentiful natural resources, unencumbered by outworn European institutions, faced with shortages of labor and capital so that the swift and the clever could rise more rapidly than almost anywhere else on earth, it was unsurprising that successful businessmen would embrace Puritanism, liberal economics, and Social Darwinism. Later, such men would find pragmatism appealing, but they were pragmatists before William James and John Dewey attempted to formulate its doctrines and beliefs. "If it works, it's good," struck a responsive chord in the business mind of the late nineteenth century.

It appeared to work. At least, it did for enough Americans to make it a national article of faith. Both urban and rural poverty existed in America, but it affected a smaller percentage of the population than in other industrializing nations of the world. Interestingly enough, only a handful of the poor and downtrodden seemed to reject the essentials of the business ideology. When they protested, they did so not in order to destroy the economic system, but to obtain their share of its benefits. Truly radical groups, such as some of the urban socialist parties of the late nineteenth and early twentieth centuries, had small followings. The Populists were radical in the American context, but their ideas were watered down and denatured by a segment of the reform Democrats. William Jennings Bryan, who today seems a reformer, was deemed a wild radical in 1896. Willing to accept the essentials of American life without much alteration, Bryan was in the extreme left wing of national politics for almost a generation. This was perhaps the best commentary on the essential acceptance of the status quo, which included the business ideology.

This ideology was formulated not by philosophers and journalists, but by businessmen themselves. Such men did not set forth a static system, but one which accepted change. In particular they welcomed those who could meet the Puritan-Social Darwinist challenge.

One of the best ways to achieve middle class status, and eventual wealth, they claimed, was through education. It had to be the proper kind of education, to be sure, combined with a good attitude toward work, and capped by faith in oneself and the system. As though to demonstrate their own faith, many businessmen supported education—of the right kind. Andrew Carnegie, who made a fortune, rewarded hard-working young men in his own companies by offering them shares in the firms, and later on gave away much of his wealth to institutions supportive of his principles; he became the spokesman for enlightened business, and was considered the leader in the movement. Carnegie appreciated the arts and humanities, but found them peripheral to a good American education. The college graduates of the past, he wrote in 1902, had been miseducated. "They have been 'educated' as if they were destined for life upon some other planet than this," he wrote. "What they have obtained has served to imbue them with false ideas and to give them a distaste for practical life." Carnegie believed he had found the proper way, not in theory, but from his own experience.

Had they gone into active work during the years spent at college they would have been better educated men in every true sense of that term. The fire and energy have been stamped out of them, and how to so manage as to live a life of idleness and not a life of usefulness has become the chief question with them.[3]

Education, then, should fit the graduate for a utilitarian existence. Culture was fine for the wealthy, who in the words of a labor leader of the 1880s were "too proud to work and too lazy to steal." But most Americans would have to learn a trade, either at the job or in the schools. Every college, wrote Joseph Medill, the probusiness editor of the Chicago *Tribune*, should have a "department of mechanism and a chemical laboratory to impart the secrets of nature and the sources of force."[4] Leland Stanford, the railroad tycoon and later governor of California, determined to endow such an institution, a memorial to his dead son.

I have been impressed with the fact that of all the young men who come to me with letters of introduction from friends in the East, the most helpless class are college men. . . . They are generally prepossessing in appearance and of good stock, but when they seek employment, and I ask them what they can do, all they can say is "anything." They have no definite technical knowledge of anything. They have no specific aim, no definite purpose. It is to overcome that condition, to give an education which shall not have that result, which I hope will be the aim of this University. . . . Its capacity to give a practical not a theoretical education ought to be accordingly foremost.[5]

Leland Stanford Junior University opened in Palo Alto, California, in the autumn of 1891. Its faculty at the time consisted of eight scholars in engineering and science, one historian (and that one being Andrew White, a specialist in the history of technology and science), and the school's president. The first student to enroll was Herbert Hoover, who would major in engineering.

The Road to Progress

The businessmen of the late nineteenth century firmly believed that true progress was possible only when artificial barriers to activity were struck down. In particular, they distrusted government. The factory owner created jobs and the worker products, while the financier enabled both to proceed with their work. The bureaucrat and politician, on the other hand, was a drone, living off the public treasury and contributing little of value in return. "Our success in resuming our place among nations and in taking the lead in paying our debts has been due to our merchants, our men of affairs, to our railroad managers, and our capitalists—far more than our statesmen," wrote Edward Atkinson, a prominent businessman of the time. Railroad tycoon Charles Elliott Perkins blasted government reformers and journalists as ". . . donkeys who can't see the operation of natural laws in fixing rates of transportation . . ."[6] Coal magnate and railroadman George F. Baer insisted that "God in His Infinite Wisdom has given control of the property interests" to directors of large corporations. To have done otherwise would have been to cripple the nation's industrial might, retard progress, and cause depression, as well as destroy liberty and freedom. William Graham Sumner, a favorite philosopher of the free-enterprisers, put the concept well in the 1880s:

> The condition for the complete and regular action of the force of competition is liberty. Liberty means the security given to each man that, if he employs his energies to sustain the struggle on behalf of himself and those he cares for, he shall dispose of the product exclusively as he chooses. . . . The human race has recognized, from the earliest times, the above conception of justice as the true one, and has founded upon it the right of property. . . . Let it be understood that we cannot go outside of this alternative: Liberty, inequality, survival of the fittest; not liberty, equality, survival of the unfittest. The former carries society forward and favors all its best members; the latter carries society downwards and favors all its worst members. . . . [7]

Businessmen did make some exceptions in their laissez faire attitude, the most obvious being the tariff. Those businessmen whose products competed with foreign goods demanded that the government erect a tariff shield for them, either to prevent foreigners from selling their wares here, or make them as expensive as the domestic products. Their justification for this stance, as in most other matters, was based on liberty. Europe was a decadent continent, they said, trapped by its feudal past, from which some—the fortunate—had escaped to come to America. The high tariff would protect American workers and businessmen from the unfair, almost slave labor of the Old World. We would take care of our own, or better still, offer them the chance to take care of themselves. Trade with Europe would be encouraged—especially the sale of American-made goods overseas. But the native market must be protected for Americans.

The concept could not be defended logically; by its very nature, trade had to be a two-way street. Furthermore, American businessmen welcomed foreign investments in railroads and industry. But logic has little to do with morality, and many businessmen of the late nineteenth century utilized moral arguments in favor of the tariff, and for that matter used them to respond to any other threat to what they deemed their well-being. [8]

American businessmen liked to contrast the free American worker to the unfree European and inferior nonwhites. This too was associated with the attitude toward government. Sumner's "forgotten man" was one who asked no help from government, preferring instead to take care of himself. Assistance from outside sources was not only deemed unnecessary, but demeaning and degrading. At times charity would be necessary but the very need was regrettable. Instead, businessmen preferred to place people in positions where they could help themselves. Assistance would be given to the unfortunate, on the clear understanding that such people, while receiving aid, were not the equals of their benefactors. This was uncomfortable to Americans, who liked to think all men were equal. Only when the recipients of such aid rejected further help—and hopefully repaid it—could they be considered worthy of reentering the society of useful Americans as equals. Carnegie, famed for his munificence, spoke often of the "Gospel of Wealth," and called upon his fellow-capitalists to use their funds to provide others with the means by which they too could rise in the social and economic order. He warned that each person had to make the ascent on his own. Carnegie believed in philanthropy, but despised charity. The former was incumbent upon the fortunate who thus repaid society as a whole; the latter was granted to individuals who, by the act of acceptance, branded themselves as inferiors.

> Those who would administer wisely must, indeed, be wise, for one of the serious obstacles to the improvement of our race is indiscriminate charity. It were better for mankind that the millions of the rich were thrown into the sea than so spent as to encourage the slothful, the drunken, the unworthy. Of every thousand dollars spent in so called charity today, it is probable that $950 is unwisely spent; so spent, indeed, as to produce the very evils which it proposes to mitigate or cure. A well-known writer of philosophical books admitted the other day that he had given a quarter of a dollar to a man who approached him as he was coming to visit the house of his friend. He knew nothing of the habits of this beggar; knew not the use that would be made of this money, although he had every reason to suspect it would be spent improperly. This man professed to be a disciple of Herbert Spencer; yet the quarter-dollar given that night will probably work more injury than all the money which its thoughtful donor will ever be able to give in true charity will do good. He only gratified his own feelings, saved himself from annoyance—and this was probably one of the most selfish and very worst actions of his life, for in all respects he is most worthy.[9]

Carnegie would give tens of millions of dollars for public libraries, but would deny a quarter to a beggar. Libraries helped people help themselves, and so furthered the cause of egalitarianism and helped produce a natural aristocracy, while the coin given the beggar encouraged the recipient to forget about honest work, and in its small way, encouraged the creation of a semifeudal attitude of noblesse oblige, with its implied concept of a permanent aristocracy.

John D. Rockefeller agreed. Charity treated the symptoms of social malaise, he thought, while proper philanthropy struck at the roots of societal problems. "The best philanthropy is constantly in search of the finalities—a search for cause, an attempt to cure evils at their source."

> The best philanthropy, the help that does the most good and the least harm, the help that nourishes civilization at its very root, that most widely disseminates health, righteousness, and happiness, is not what is usually called charity. It is, in my judgment, the investment of effort or time or money, carefully considered with relation to the power of employing people at a remunerative wage, to expand and develop the resources at hand, and to give opportunity for progress and healthful labour where it did not exist before. No mere money-giving is comparable to this in its lasting and beneficial results.[10]

Let Carnegie endow libraries and aid educational institutions. Rockefeller would expand his business, providing jobs for his workers. This too would be doing God's work on earth, and further the cause of democracy. On one occasion, Rockefeller compared Standard Oil to an American beauty rose, which, in order to flourish, pushed lesser blooms from the soil and, in effect, destroyed them. Taken together, these two statements appear to provide a rationale not only for large-scale business, but for the humane and philanthropic life. By achieving success, the businessman makes it possible for those employed by him to earn the good life for themselves. This must be earned; dignity, pride, and satisfaction could not be bestowed as a Christian act on the part of the giver, but rather must be sweated for, and viewed as a sign of competence on the part of the worker.

Once this view is accepted, it can be seen there is no true contention between the employer and employee. The latter wants to be more like the former than he is; the employer works hard to retain his position and expand upon it. Both accept the rules of the game, even though they have received different rewards in the playing. Each serves the other as well, and in the Rockefeller view, both work in harmony for the greater good of society as a whole.

This is not to say that businessmen believed competition was wholly desirable. Winners in the race like Rockefeller and Carnegie could extol its virtues, but what of the losers? The economy of the late nineteenth and early twentieth centuries seemed certain to produce a large crop of these.

Overproduction was a nagging problem in this period. The domestic market was not growing rapidly enough to absorb increases in productivity. Higher wages might have alleviated the situation, but businessmen, faced with declining profits, were in no mood to accept such a solution. Foreign competition was fierce, and although American exports were increasing, volume was not keeping pace with productivity either. If Adam Smith spoke to the positive side of such a situation (for the winners) David Ricardo, in the early nineteenth century, evaluated the predicament for the losers. Competition could cripple the system, producing a situation in which no one really won. This seemed to be the situation for small and medium sized businesses in the Rockefeller-Carnegie era.

Rather than cut prices in the Ricardian manner, a solution most considered destructive, such businessmen opted instead to unite to "regularize" markets and dampen if not eliminate competition. For some this took the form of holding companies, trusts, gentlemen's agreements, and the like. Others turned to industrial associations, chambers of commerce, the National Association of Manufacturers, and other organizations of like-minded businessmen which would lobby for legislation, help elect friendly politicians to office, and agree with one another to accept mutual restraints.

Men in small and medium sized businesses took eagerly to the associational idea. "There is not a manufacturer in the country who is not an organizational man in theory and daily practice," said James W. Van Cleave of the National Association of Manufacturers, while John Kirby, Jr., also of that organization, added, "We are living in an age of organization, an age when organization must cope with organization; an age when organization alone can preserve your individual freedom and mine." And the organizational idea abounded. By 1908 James Couzens of Ford Motor refused to join another. What we need, he said, was "an Association of Associations. There are too many Associations now."[11]

Competition and Cooperation

The Social Darwinists had claimed that competition—unrestrained competition at that—was natural and beneficial; businessmen eagerly accepted the idea and used it for their own ends. But increasingly the economic realities were indicating that cooperation was necessary, an obvious violation of Social Darwinist dictates. This contradiction did not seem to bother most businessmen, who simply ignored it. Instead, they set about creating a new rationale for cooperation. Efficiency would be promoted when businessmen got together to share information and end wasteful competition said some, while others claimed that unity of business was needed in the face of the threat from organized labor and "radicals" and "socialists." When the progressives obtained influence and power in Washington, and embarked upon what on the surface at least appeared an anti-big business campaign, businessmen responded by claiming that unity was needed to oppose the threat from that quarter too. Elbert Gary, president of United States Steel, sponsored the so-called Gary dinners, occasions when the steel makers would meet socially and professionally to carve up the market and set prices. Gary observed that the dinners were not violations of law. "The law does not compel competition; it only prohibits an agreement not to compete." Gary claimed no such agreements had been made. "The movement has been simply an effort . . . to establish a basis of friendly association and intercourse which is calculated to enable each to obtain full knowledge concerning the affairs of all the others and the beneficial results which naturally follow such knowledge." The agreements were informal; they placed each man under an "obligation of honor . . . even stronger than the obligation of an agreement."[12]

The associational movement received additional impetus from the need to unite in reaction to business dislocations in the early twentieth century. The clash between James Hill and J.P. Morgan on the one hand and E.H. Harriman and Jacob Schiff on the other regarding the western railroads resulted in a short-lived panic in 1901. In 1903, there was another minor dislocation. But in 1907 a far more serious crash took place, due in part to shaky financing, overexpansion, and manipulations. This time not only weak companies were liquidated, but the strong as well. Were it not for Morgan's ability to unite the bankers behind him—in effect, forming an ad hoc association—the nation's credit might have been destroyed. President Roosevelt recognized the dangers inherent in the situation. Not only did he sanction the bankers' consortium, but he cooperated with it, to the extent of ordering his treasury department to take orders from Morgan until the crisis was resolved.[13]

Government-business cooperation continued during the rest of the Roosevelt administration. Woodrow Wilson promised to end it shortly prior to coming to office in 1913, but a recession that year led him to moderate his stance. Wilson rejected a business-sponsored proposal for a central bank, which would have been under the direction of Wall Street, and instead supported the Federal Reserve System, itself a compromise between Wall

Streeters and those who would smash the "Money Trust." The president hoped the new bank would be independent of business in general and Wall Street in particular. Then, as though to mitigate the situation, he named business representatives to key positions at the Federal Reserve. Benjamin Strong, one of the first governors of the New York Federal Reserve Bank, head of that bank through most of the 1920s and the most powerful central banker in the nation during this period, came out of the Morgan-dominated Bankers Trust Company.[14] Wilson, no less than his Republican successors, named businessmen to the Federal Reserve Board.

The always halfhearted conflict between government and business came to a temporary halt with the outbreak of World War I in 1914. President Wilson informally suspended the antitrust laws and soon after called upon businessmen to assist in the preparedness effort. In 1916, a year prior to the American declaration of war, Congress voted to establish a Council of National Defense, consisting of members of the cabinet and a civilian advisory panel, which included Howard Coffin of Hudson Motor Company, Walter Gifford of American Telephone and Telegraph, Julius Rosenwald of Sears-Roebuck, and private speculator Bernard Baruch. Wilson hoped the council would coordinate the various segments of the economy and prepare for full mobilization when and if it were needed. The call was clear:

> One of the objects of the Council will be to inform American manufacturers as to the part they can play in the national emergency. It is empowered to establish at once and maintain through subordinate bodies of specially qualified persons an auxiliary organization composed of men of the best creative and administrative capacity, capable of mobilizing to the utmost the resources of the country.[15]

Later on Baruch was named head of the War Industries Board, which coordinated the war effort. The WIB, acting for government but composed largely of businessmen, was the most powerful civilian agency operating on the home front, while Baruch was deemed by many the nation's most influential figure after the president.

The government-business partnership, cemented in war, added another element to the business ideology. Prior to the war, government actions were considered an unnatural interference in the workings of society, necessary perhaps, but certainly not on the same level of "productive labor." During the progressive period some businessmen viewed government as a conspiracy to destroy capitalism in one way or another, and at worst, the agency through which America would become socialist. Now, for the first time, businessmen not only controlled politicians or fought them, but operated as bureaucrats themselves. They came to realize that government had its uses, not as an agency to help business expand (often at the expense of other segments of society), but as an integral part of a highly complex and interrelated social and economic organism.

The doctrine of competition, already hallowed, would continue to receive lip service, and would be extolled at business and public meetings. But in practice it would often be ignored. The associational philosophy would be encouraged, and become the subject of numerous books and magazine articles. Government would also play its role, and in some ways one more significant than that of the associations though often it would work in harmony with them. It would create and encourage the proper climate for associations, passing legislation to enforce necessary rules and punishing those who transgressed them, and coordinating the national economy. In this way, the men of the 1890s began to come to terms with the realities that would mark the 1920s (*Alternative 1:* see Document 1).

This adjustment needed two more elements before the seal could be made permanent. The first was an ideology that would legitimize the end of true laissez faire, and offer a rationale for the change to cooperation and the use of government. The second was a test of the new nexus, one that would satisfy everyone that the new business civilization in the making was pragmatically sound—that it would work.

Both elements developed and became part of the business creed in the aftermath of the war.

The ideology was anti-Bolshevist, based on fear that the Soviet revolution in Russia was only the first step in a plan to seize control of the world, with the United States targeted for a quick takeover. There seemed ample evidence that such a conspiracy existed. First there was the revolution itself, in 1917, with Leon Trotsky claiming it as the first step toward the communization of Europe. Then, in 1918-1919, the United States was hit by a wave of strikes. Some labor leaders used radical rhetoric, frightening a middle class already troubled by thoughts of revolution. The New York clothing workers went out late in 1918, followed by the longshoremen. There was a general strike in Seattle early in 1919, then a walkout of telephone workers in New England. A railroad strike paralyzed some major lines, and Boston was hit by a police strike later in the year. In September the workers at U.S. Steel staged their walkout.

The situation seemed grim. In fact, there were fewer strikes in either 1918 or 1919 than in 1917, and the vast majority of these concerned wages and hours. In the mind of the public, however, the 1918-1919 strikes were linked with the Russian Revolution, and its export to the United States.

The Socialist party did well in the 1917 and 1918 elections. In New York the party polled twenty-seven percent of the vote for mayor, while in Chicago the figure was thirty-four percent, and forty-four percent in Dayton. This too was not unusual, for the Socialist vote had been growing prior to the war. But added to the strikes, it posed a fearful prospect for middle class America.

One reaction was the famous "Red Raids" of the late Wilson Administration. Led by Attorney General A. Mitchell Palmer, federal agents instituted a campaign against radicals, real and imaginary, that lasted two years. To some, it seemed a replay of early twentieth-century Russia, with the Socialists and other radicals playing the Bolshevik role, and Palmer and his men that of the secret police. Palmer did what he could to keep this fear alive. Writing in 1920, he said:

Like a prairie-fire, the blaze of revolution was sweeping over every American institution of law and order a year ago. It was eating its way into the homes of the American workman, its sharp tongues of revolutionary heat were licking the alters of the churches, leaping into the belfry of the school bell, crawling into the sacred corners of American homes, seeking to replace marriage vows with libertine laws, burning up the foundations of society.[16]

There were bomb scares in 1920, several directed against businessmen. In September a wagonload of explosives was set off outside the Wall Street offices of J.P. Morgan and Co., killing thirty-eight and causing $2 million in damage. Then, before the shock could be digested, race riots erupted in northern cities. This was additional evidence of Bolshevik activity, or at least it seemed so to many, especially those in the business community.

There was never a danger of revolution in the United States, but it would have been difficult to convince many middle class and wealthy businessmen that this was so. Businessmen realized that if capitalism was swept away in a Soviet-style revolution, they would be the first to go. Even after the fear subsided in the early 1920s, a residue remained as businessmen and business-oriented politicians cast wary eyes on the U.S.S.R. Could it happen here? Some thought it might. To prevent the communization of America, businessmen sought means to defend the United States. Attempts would have to be made to define American capitalism, and especially to contrast it with the ideology of the Soviet Union. Just as Soviet Russia seemed a united, rational camp, so the United States would have to become more unified, and business more rational. Free enterprise—at least of the variety American businessmen had extolled in the late nineteenth century—seemed destructive. It meant Americans were competing with Americans, when they should unite to fight the Soviets. Now the cooperation that business had practiced in that period (in opposition to what they had proclaimed) seemed even more desirable, not only in day-to-day activities, but as part of the business creed. The close government-business cooperation of 1914-1919, necessary then to defend the nation during a wartime emergency, was now supported on the grounds that it would still further unite America against all varieties of radicals.

No sooner had this new rationale developed than was it tested. The nation entered a depression in the spring of 1920 that lasted until late the following year.

The causes of the depression seemed clear enough. Within hours of the November 11, 1917 armistice, the War Industry Board announced an end to overtime and Sunday work on federal orders. During the next three weeks more than $2.5 billion worth of unfilled orders were cancelled, and more followed. At the same time plans for the discharge of two million servicemen were put into operation. These jolts were expected to trigger an economic decline, but despite government mishandling of conversion efforts, none came. Pent-up consumer demands and the need to continue relief work served to dampen deflationary tendencies for a while, and even produced an unexpected postwar boom.

The crash came in 1920, during the presidential election campaign. The banking system, having reached its legal limits of credit expansion, began restricting loans. There was a market for agricultural goods, but would-be purchasers lacked credit to pay the inflated prices. Business suffered for the same reason. Surpluses were thrown on the market, and prices slumped rapidly. In 1919-1920 there were more than thirty thousand bankruptcies, almost five hundred thousand farm foreclosures, and five million unemployed workers. In January, 1921, the unemployment rate stood at twenty percent. The gross national product, which reached a record peak of $88.9 billion in 1920, declined to $74 billion in 1921.

There had been periodic depressions in the past. Indeed, in 1921 the business cycle was considered as unalterable as the law of supply and demand. One accepted the benefits of the boom, and then paid for them by suffering through the bust. Democratic presidential candidate James Cox said little about it. Republican Warren Harding said that if he were elected, he would raise the tariff to protect farmers, cut income taxes, and hold federal spending in line. Hoover, who campaigned for Harding, agreed with this plan. But the major issues in the election were the League of Nations and prohibition.

The recovery, which began in 1922, came more rapidly than expected. The Federal Reserve reversed its tight money policy in May, demand caught up with supply, and prices firmed. Led by tax cuts, cheap money, and large scale capital spending programs, the nation entered a seven year boom, one of the greatest it had ever known, and certainly the most famous in its history.

The Synthesis of 1921

In September, 1921, President Harding convened a Conference on Unemployment "to consider relief for four or five million unemployed resulting from the business slump of 1921." The conference was planned by such prominent individuals as Owen D. Young, chairman of the board of General Electric, former president Joseph H. Defrees of the U.S. Chamber of Commerce, Matthew Woll of the American Federation of Labor, and Clarence M. Woolley, president of the American Radiator Company. Among the participants were some of the nation's most prominent economists, including Wesley C. Mitchell of the National Bureau of Economic Research, Paul Brissenden of Columbia University, Ernest Bradford of the American Statistical Association, Thomas Sewall Adams of Yale, and Leo Wolman of the New School of Social Research.

The conference went beyond its original mandate. Unemployment was discussed, but far more time was taken in an analysis of the business cycle. Throughout almost all the papers delivered there ran a thread of inevitability. Business cycles were natural, they followed patterns, they could be studied scientifically, and possibly their effects could be mitigated. Frederick R. Macaulay of the National Bureau wrote:

> ... there is evidence that certain crises and certain revivals have started in one district and spread gradually over the rest of the country. For example the panic of 1907 appears to have begun in New York City

and to have radiated from there to other financial centers. . . . Similarly, the sudden revival in the autumn of 1891 was first noted in the wheat-growing areas. The "granger" railroads reported an increase of profits some months before the lines in other districts experienced a revival. Finally, there is a wide diversity of fortunes at the same time and in the same trade among different business enterprises. In every year of deep depression an occasional concern reports that it has had "the best season in history." And it is notorious that there is never a year, no matter how prosperous, when hundreds of businessmen to not go bankrupt.[17]

Macauley's article, and others like it, indicate that economists were becoming convinced that depressions could be dissected, almost like cadavers, and that general knowledge of them might be obtained sometime in the future. This knowledge could then be used to "cure" depressions. Wesley Mitchell, a pioneer in the field, wrote a scientifically-oriented paper for the committee, which contained paragraphs giving that impression.[18] In writing of the end of depressions, he used generic rather than specific language:

Once these various forces have set the physical volume of trade to expanding again, the increase proves cumulative, though for a time the pace of growth is kept slow by the continued sagging of prices. But while the latter maintains the pressure upon business men and prevents the increased volume of orders from producing a rapid rise of profits, still business prospects become gradually brighter. Old debts have been paid, accumulated stocks of commodities have been absorbed, weak enterprises have been reorganized, the banks are strong—all the clouds upon the financial horizon have disappeared. Everything is ready for a revival of activity, which will begin whenever some fortunate circumstance gives a sudden fillip to demand, or, in the absence of such an event, when the slow growth of the volume of business has filled order books and paved the way for a new rise in profits.[19]

Nowhere in the conference report did a business economist suggest the federal government take the lead in bringing the nation out of a depression. The government could advise, encourage, help bring people together, and in other ways create an atmosphere of confidence. But the patient would have to rely upon time and the natural unfolding of economic laws for his eventual recovery. One participant, Otto T. Mallery of the Pennsylvania State Industrial Board, suggested that federal works projects might be manipulated in such a way as to create jobs, but even he placed more of the burden on cities and states than on Washington.

The Foreword to the report was written by Secretary of Commerce Herbert Hoover. In it he stated:

Broadly, the business cycle is a constant recurrence of irregularly separated booms and slumps. The general conclusion of the Committee is that the slumps are in the main due to the wastes, extravagance, speculation, inflation, over-expansion, and inefficiency in production developed during the booms, the strategic point of attack, therefore, is the reduction of these evils, mainly through the provision for such current economic information as will show the sign of danger, and its more general understanding and use by producers, distributors, and banks, inducing more constructive and safer policies.

Hoover did not regard the report as a mere theoretical document. Rather, he issued a call to action, one he hoped the business community would accept.

> The report does not suggest panaceas or economic revolution but seeks to drive home the facts that the enlargement of judgement in individual business men as to the trend of business and consequent widened vision as to the approaching dangers will greatly contribute to stability, and that the necessary information upon which such judgements can be based must be systematically recruited and distributed.[20]

Knowledge, then, is power. Once the businessman learns what must be done in order to create a healthy business environment, he will act. Science, logic, self-interest, intelligence—that was all that was needed to assure prosperity and the continued flourishing of the American people. The nation had come through that test in the depression of 1921 and had received few scars and acquired much knowledge in the process.

By then the men of the early 1920s, who had come of age at the turn of the century and had drunk deeply from the springs of laissez faire faith, had incorporated the associational ideas, anticommunism, scientism, and the belief in government-business cooperation into their creed. Competition and harmony, science and morality, pragmatism and patriotism, coexisted, without apparent difficulty, in the business mind of the 1920s. And that business mind had not only an exemplar and hero, but a philosopher and leader in Herbert Hoover, who more than anyone else combined the old ideas with the new in what appeared a satisfactory mix (*Alternative 2:* see Document 2).

Notes

1. Those who seem to think in terms of decades often seek single figures, usually a president, who somehow typifies the period. Franklin D. Roosevelt filled the bill for the 1930s, Dwight Eisenhower for the 1950s, William McKinley for the 1890s, and probably Lyndon Johnson, not John Kennedy, will be used as a symbol for the 1960s. The 1920s, in contrast, offers three sharply different men as symbols, and each for a different aspect of the period. Warren Harding was supposed to stand for the desire to return to the simple, McKinleyesque past. Newspaper editors and popular historians used William Allen White's description of Coolidge as a "Puritan in Babylon," and contrasted him with the men and women of the jazz age. Herbert Hoover, the most popular American to emerge from World War I, was called the "Great Engineer" through most of the decade, an indication of the growth of industrialization. Later on he came to symbolize failure—the flaws and inadequacies of the decade. Actually, such delineations are unfair to all these presidents. None began their life, or even became prominent, in a year ending in zero, and then faded away ten years later.

2. Robert S. Lynd and Helen M. Lynd, *Middletown: A Study in Modern American Culture* (New York: Harcourt, Bruce and World, 1956), pp. 28-29.

3. Andrew Carnegie, *The Empire of Business* (New York: Doubleday, Page and Co., 1902), pp. 145-47.

4. Edward C. Kirkland, *Dream and Thought in the Business Community, 1860-1900* (Ithaca, N.Y.: Cornell University Press, 1956), pp. 87-90.

5. O.L. Elliott, *Stanford University: The First Twenty-Five Years* (Stanford: Stanford University Press, 1937), pp. 19-20.

6. Kirkland, *Dream and Thought*, pp. 23-24.

7. Albert G. Keller and Maurice R. Davie, eds., *Essays of William Graham Sumner* (New Haven: Yale University Press, 1934), Vol. II, pp. 93-95.

8. Even Louis Brandeis, considered a radical in some circles, who vigorously opposed the tarriff, echoed pro-business sentiments on occasion, and in such a way as to indicate his essential moderation. "I am strenuously opposed to the Government fixing any price in any business that is competitive," wrote antitrust advocate Brandeis, "but I do think that a man who has an individual article, whether it be covered by a patent, copyright, trade-mark, or trade-name—something which is known as his article—should have the right to have that article distributed under the conditions he deems best, including a fixed price, provided always that it is a competitive article; that is, that the field of competition is left open. . . . It is in the interest of the community that a man in free business, in a competitive business, shall have the incentive to make just as much money as he can. If he makes too much money—I mean according to these economic doctrines—he is sure to find some fellow coming in and trying to share it with him." Brandeis was never able to square his belief in free enterprise with his reform views. Alfred Lief, ed., *The Social and Economic Views of Mr. Justice Brandeis* (New York: Vanguard, 1930), pp. 402-403.

9. Andrew Carnegie, "Wealth," *North American Review* 257 (1889): 659-60.

10. John D. Rockefeller, *Random Reminiscences of Men and Events* (New York: Doubleday, Doran and Co., 1937), pp. 141-42.

11. Robert H. Wiebe, *Businessmen and Reform: A Study of the Progressive Movement* (Cambridge, Mass.: Harvard University Press, 1962), pp. 18, 33.

12. Ibid., pp. 83-84.

13. Robert Sobel, *Panic on Wall Street: A History of America's Financial Disasters* (New York: Macmillan, 1968), pp. 297-321.

14. Lester V. Chandler, *Benjamin Strong: Central Banker* (Washington: Brookings Institution, 1958).

15. Grosvener Clarkson, *Industrial America in the World War* (New York: Houghton Mifflin, 1923), pp. 21-22.

16. A. Mitchell Palmer, "The Case Against the Reds," *The Forum* 63 (1920): 174.

17. *Business Cycles and Unemployment: Report and Recommendations of a Committee of the President's Conference on Unemployment, Including an Investigation Made Under the Auspices of the National Bureau of Economic Research* (New York: McGraw-Hill, 1923), p. 19.

18. See Wesley C. Mitchell, *Business Cycles: The Problem and its Setting* (New York: National Bureau of Economic Research, Inc., 1927), for the best statement of Mitchell's creed.

19. *Business Cycles and Unemployment*, p. 18.

20. Ibid., p. vi.

2

A Businessman in Babylon

In 1928, when the prosperity of the "New Era" was at its apogee, Democrat Alfred E. Smith contested Republican Herbert C. Hoover for the presidency. On their records both men appeared able, and throughout the campaign they showed a decent respect for one another, even while their supporters engaged in some of the most vicious mud-slinging in American electoral history. There were many campaign issues, but Smith concentrated on agricultural policy and Republican favoritism to big business. Hoover tended to speak in generalities, praising outgoing President Coolidge and delivering long, rather boring technical speeches on some of the issues.

The Great Engineer was much admired (Alternative 3: see Documents 3-a-3-b), but there were those who had doubts. "The central fact militating against Candidate Hoover is that many people cannot understand what he stands for," wrote *Time* magazine. "A technologist, he does not discuss ultimate purposes. In a society of temperate, industrious, unspeculative beavers, such a beaver-man would make an ideal King-beaver. But humans are different. People want Herbert Hoover to tell where, with his extraordinary abilities, he would lead them." Perhaps unwittingly the writer perceptively concluded that Hoover needed "to undergo a spiritual crisis before he will satisfy as a popular leader."[1]

Samuel Crowther, in an adulatory campaign book on Hoover, thought Hoover's outlook—that of science rather than politics—just what the country needed in the New Era.

> In the old way of thinking, only three professions were learned—law, medicine and theology. But only one profession was wholly respectable, and that was soldiering. Government has been mostly in the hands of soldiers and lawyers. Now we have a government by lawyers. But our material progress is and has been in the hands of scientists, engineers, business men, and financiers. If we define engineering as the "art of directing the great sources of power in nature for the use and convenience of man," then all of those who are helping in the development of the country may qualify as engineers.[2]

And Hoover, of course, was the greatest of them all. Of this, few had doubts, even those who planned to vote for Smith.

In any case Smith, not Hoover, was the issue in 1928. He was the first Catholic nominated for the presidency by a major party, and he opposed prohibition, that crusade which, though faltering, still had many followers. Journalists questioned Smith's qualifications on both grounds, and predicted they would divide the party, as they had in 1924, resulting in a Republican victory. The question raised by *Time* was all but forgotten by election day. It did not seem important at the time.

Hoover won a smashing victory, receiving 444 electoral votes to 87, capturing 40 states to 9, with 21.5 million popular votes to Smith's 15 million. He received 58.2 percent of the popular vote, a margin only slightly lower than that granted Harding in his record 1920 victory. No candidate had ever received a larger electoral total. Hoover rolled up record pluralities in districts that were normally Republican, and for the first time since Reconstruction, a Republican received votes from the states of the former Confederacy. There were indications that many soldiers who had fought alongside Lee and Jackson had cast their ballots for a man nominated by the party of Lincoln and Grant.

It had been an unusual election campaign, capped by remarkable results. In their analysis of it, newspapermen and political commentators stressed the religious and prohibition issues. Journalists, noting the prosperity of the country, concluded that any Democrat would have lost, and wondered whether the Republicans could ever be dislodged from the White House.

At no time did the journalists attempt to contrast the backgrounds and qualifications of the two candidates. Even Smith's managers failed to do so, perhaps because they were too busy with the other issues. The Hoover staff, realizing its man would win easily, said little. Had they done so, the public might have realized that Smith—the first urban candidate in the nation's history as well as the first Catholic—was in the traditional mold of presidential hopefuls. As the governor of a large state, and a man with considerable political experience, his election would not have been so out-of-the-ordinary as most believed at the time. Of the six presidents elected in the twentieth century to that time, four had served as governors of their states, while a fifth, Harding, had been a senator. Only William Howard Taft had failed to occupy either position, and his lack of political acumen was famous.

Herbert Hoover: The New Breed

Hoover was of a different breed. One could hardly have called him a politician at all in 1928, even though he had handled himself well in the 1920s. More than Smith, he was an exotic in the American political tradition. Never before or since has a man with his unusual background been elected to the presidency.

Hoover was the first Quaker to become president. Had the Democrats nominated a wet Protestant in 1928, they might have raised the religious issue against him. As it was, they could scarcely afford to discuss it without bringing instant retaliation from the Republicans.

Hoover was the only president whose primary occupation prior to entering government service had been in business.[3] He was known as "the Great Engineer," but in fact his professional reputation was based more on his organizational abilities, financial acumen, and business sense, than on any engineering feat or discovery. Hoover had been trained as a technician, but for most of his business life, he functioned as an organizer and financier.

With the exception of military officers who became president—and not all of these—Hoover was the only president whose first electoral office was the presidency itself. Even Taft had once won election as a state judge, while Chester A. Arthur was elected as vice-president in his first canvas.

No president in American history, before or since, has spent so much of his time abroad. In 1897, at the age of twenty-three, Hoover set off for an engineering position in Australia. Most of his next twenty-three years were spent overseas, usually in relatively primitive areas of Australia, Africa, and Asia. In one of these years (1898) Hoover was unable to return to the United States even for a visit. He knew more of the world from firsthand experience than almost any other American of his generation, and no president, even those of the jet age, could match his background. On the other hand, Hoover knew little of the United States until he entered federal service in the Wilson administration in 1917.

Hoover was the first "rootless" man to become president.[4] Each of his predecessors had been identified with a state. Hoover had been born in Iowa, moved to Oregon at the age of ten, was in California at seventeen, and travelled through the American West at twenty-one. Later on he purchased a cottage at Stanford—in effect making his alma mater his home—while maintaining quarters in New York and London as well.

Hoover was a shy man by nature, and found it difficult to make friends. This difficulty was compounded by the nature of his business career. He spent much of his time dealing with individuals he considered his inferiors, such as Australian or Burmese workers or nonwestern potentates. He was good at his job, but in all his long foreign career, failed to become truly friendly with any oriental or Australian businessman or politician or, for that matter, with many Europeans. Early on, Hoover developed an imperial point of view, one which had more in common with the men of the British Raj than with anything to be found in the American experience. After all, Americans spoke of the white man's burden, from a poem Rudyard Kipling had written, to celebrate the Spanish-American War. But Hoover actually experienced the burden. So he moved through the world, isolated and alone, except for his colleagues. Even with them, there was little in the way of friendship to be found. Hoover's close associates admired him, respected him, and in the case of a few, idolized him. But only a few actually liked him as a person, or so it would seem from the memoirs available.

Almost every president brought a group of cronies to the White House with him—Harding's Ohio Gang, Kennedy's Irish Mafia, and Eisenhower's businessman friends are only a few examples. Hoover had few such individuals upon whom to draw. Rarely would the Hoovers dine alone, however. Always there seemed someone or some group to be entertained. Hoover was a cordial host, and afterwards talk would turn to business matters. In effect, these were more business meetings than social events. Later, it would be said that Franklin Roosevelt had many friends, but even more former friends, while Hoover had few friends, but no former friends. This was not really the case. Roosevelt stirred strong feelings among those who knew him because, more than most presidents, he allowed himself to be known. Hoover had a small number of friends, most of whom, like Will Irwin, were college chums—the last time Hoover would meet people on equal terms for many years was at Stanford—and a devoted legion of admirers.

Hoover was one of those rare individuals who feel no strong need for recreation. Most previous presidents managed to find time for relaxation, if only to "recharge their mental batteries." Not Hoover, who broke sharply with the practice of his predecessors in working long hours, night and day, and even weekends. In this respect Hoover was the first full-time president the nation had; not even Lincoln, during the Civil War, was at the presidential desk for longer stretches. Hoover did have one mania: fresh water fishing. He managed to keep it in check most of the time. Later on, when advisors told him it would improve his image to be seen at play, Hoover went on fishing trips, and did relax on occasion.[5] But he gave sighs of relief when they were over, and he could get back to work. Ike Hoover, chief usher of the White House and no relation to Herbert Hoover, served every president from Harrison to Franklin Roosevelt, and seemed to like Hoover the least. His remarks have to be read in that light. "President Hoover," he wrote, "was unusually sensitive to newspaper criticism."

> He did not like the publishing of news about his fishing trips, and this consideration kept him at home many times. He felt that the people would think he was neglecting his duty. In this he differed greatly from some of his predecessors who felt they could do as they pleased when they were President. His devotion to duty made it hard, of course, on the employees about the place, who got but little chance to relax. They worked Sundays, holidays, and many extra hours. The Hoovers worked hard themselves and thought everybody else should do the same.

"Hoover seemed to feel that he would be unfavorably criticized if he took a vacation," concluded Ike Hoover. "He reminded me of a fellow who was always afraid of losing his job and must hang around in an effort to hold on."[6]

Later it would be suggested that Hoover's attitude toward work and his apparent uncertainty on several key occasions was due to the fact that he had been a poor boy, an orphan, who through hard work and determination, had risen to the top. Often such individuals demonstrate uncertainty in social situations, and continue their infatuation with work long after the need for it has passed. Journalists in the 1920s and 1930s, influenced by popular psychology, claimed that the "Horatio Alger syndrome" drove him on. Even Hoover talked of a rise from rags to riches on occasion.[7] But this was not the case: Hoover had never known real poverty.

Hoover's creed did not emerge from a poor childhood and hard struggle against the odds. Rather, it came from the gradual incorporation of the business ideology. In part this derived from reading. Though not interested in economics in college, he spent a good deal of time while travelling by reading the works of Adam Smith, David Ricardo, John Stuart Mill, and Walter Bagehot. More important, however, were his experiences and observations, most of which were overseas.[8] Hoover believed himself a typical American businessman, even though he had little direct contact with American business. The combination of experiences in Australia and Asia, combined with readings in classical economics and a sparse knowledge of America, provided fertile soil for acceptance of the words, not the deeds, of men like Carnegie and Rockefeller. Having settled upon the creed, Hoover seemed content with it. He would maintain it for the rest of his long life, ignoring internal contradictions, often blinding himself to its outworn nature in the post-1929 period.

Hoover's Years of Preparation

Hoover was born in West Branch, Iowa, on August 10, 1874. His father, Jesse Hoover, was a blacksmith and farm implements dealer. His mother, Hulda Hoover, was a teacher who was also very active in local Quaker affairs, and who inculcated the faith in her sons, Theodore and Herbert, and her daughter May. Later, Hoover would recall that his childhood was filled with moral lessons; most importantly that hard work was rewarded and diligence prized. But it was also enjoyable; Hoover had a happy childhood. Writing of this period in 1951, at the age of seventy-seven, he said:

> I prefer to think of Iowa as I saw it through the eyes of a ten-year old boy. Those were eyes filled with the wonders of Iowa's streams and woods, of the mystery of growing crops. They saw days filled with adventure and great undertakings, with participation in good and comforting things. They saw days of stern but kindly discipline.[9]

As a boy, Hoover was taken to many Quaker meetings, and although never very religious in an outward sense, for the rest of his life Hoover would reflect the early lessons he had learned. In 1932 a fellow Quaker, attempting to interpret him through an understanding of the religion, wrote:

> Instead of a formal creed, the Quakers, or Religious Society of Friends, place first of all a belief in the Inner Light, or Christ Within. This Inner Light they hold more important than the written Scriptures, and, among many Quakers, than the historical Christ. Strict integrity in business transactions is enjoined, a constant carefully keeping of accounts, truth and sincerity of speech, without omission or exaggeration; but one's work should be done with conscientious enthusiasm, and this can be stretched a long way. And, over all and supreme over all earthly and supernatural matters is the man's own Inner Light. We will find Herbert Hoover moving under this glow.[10]

It was a religious tradition which placed man in the midst of his community, and called upon him to serve this community well, but reserved for the individual all moral judgments. Even if all oppose you, and you have received a vision of the Inner Light, you must follow it. This perhaps was admirable in a saint, but hardly the kind of creed a politician could hold for long if he were to survive in the world of compromise.

Jesse Hoover died of typhoid fever in 1880, and three years later Hulda Hoover died of pneumonia. At the age of nine, young Herbert went to live on the farm of his paternal uncle, Allan Hoover, near West Branch, while his brother went to the farm of another uncle and his sister to the home of his maternal grandmother. Never again would they be close. The Quaker community in West Branch was warm and generous, but it could scarcely have compensated for the family taken from the young boy so quickly.

After a year with Allan Hoover, Herbert travelled to Newberg, Oregon, where he lived with a maternal uncle, Dr. Henry J. Minthorn. He went to Friend's Pacific Academy, a Quaker school Dr. Minthorn had helped found, and worked at odd jobs after school, not so much for the money as because Hoover even then considered remunerative work to be good in itself. In 1888 the Minthorns moved to Salem, Oregon, and took Herbert with them. Dr. Minthorn opened a land settlement business there and Hoover, while going to school, worked as office boy and general assistant after hours.

Dr. Minthorn had hoped Hoover would enroll at a Quaker college, and had obtained for him a scholarship at Earlham in Indiana. But by then Hoover had determined to become an engineer, and applied instead for admission to Stanford, which he attended from 1891 to 1895, graduating with an A.B. degree.

Those who remember Hoover at Stanford recall a shy young man, who rarely spoke except when spoken to, and then replied with only a few words. He worked his way through college, delivering newspapers to other boys and collecting laundry, and during the summers would seek employment in the field, obtaining funds as well as experience. He did join with the "barbarians" who opposed the fraternity groups at the new university, and even ran for office, that of financial manager, and won. Hoover handled the funds efficiently, so much so that he earned the dislike of the more easygoing students, especially when he insisted that lost footballs be paid for by those responsible. Indeed, he was so efficient that he managed to show a profit for the sports program, a rarity then and later on.

Hoover was anything but a Frank Merriwell type of student. He had entered Stanford to receive an education, and he got what he wanted. This is not to say he did not enjoy himself, but rather that his joys were the quiet ones, to be savored by oneself, and not as part of a group. Later on he would say his years at Stanford were among the happiest of his life, to the slight surprise of some who had gone through college with him. One of his teachers, Dr. Vernon Kellogg, recalled that Hoover was only interested in those subjects that would make him a better engineer. "He would start in on a course, and then, if he found it unpromising as a contribution to the special education in which he was interested, he would simply drop out of the class without consultation or permission.[11] Another professor, a devout Quaker named Joseph Swain, recalled that Hoover, as a would-be freshman, lacked the preparation in mathematics needed for entry. He studied day and night on his own to acquire the necessary background to pass the entrance examinations.

> I observed that he put his teeth together with great decision, and his whole face and posture showed his determination to pass the examinations at any cost. He evidently was summoning every pound of energy he possessed to answer correctly the questions before him. I was

naturally interested in him. On inquiry I learned that he had studied only two books of Plane Geometry, and was trying to solve an original problem based on the fourth book. While he was unable to do this, he did much better; for the intelligence and superior will he revealed in the attempt convinced me that such a boy needed only to be given a chance. So although he could not pass all of the tests, I told him to come to my rooms at the hotel after the examinations, as I would like to talk with him. He came promptly at the appointed hour with a friend of his, the son of a banker in Salem, Oregon. The two boys invited me and Mrs. Swain to visit them, which we did. I learned there that Herbert Hoover, for that was the boy's name, was an industrious, thoughtful, ambitious boy earning his own living.[11]

Industrious, thoughtful, and ambitious—not bright, original, or exceptional—were the kinds of words that came to mind when thinking of Hoover in this period. Like the Horatio Alger hero, he applied himself to problems, and would not rest until they were solved. This was possible in engineering, and so Hoover came to believe it would be the same in other fields of endeavor. The hard-working president, attempting to find solutions to the political, social, and economic complexities of the Great Depression, had his origin in the young engineering student at Stanford.[12] But these problems of fear and uncertainty were not of the kind that would lend themselves to scientific solutions, at least not unless the science were alloyed with art. This was something Hoover did not understand at the time, came to realize intellectually later on, but could never accept emotionally.[13]

After graduation, Hoover worked for a while for the U.S. Geological Survey, an experience which took him through the West, and taught him to have contempt for "damn bureaucrats."[14] Then, in 1897, he received an offer from the prestigious British mining firm of Bewick, Moreing & Company, to work at an engineering project in Australia. Hoover accepted, set off for London to meet with the partners, came to an agreement, and went off to the gold fields of Australia.[15]

Hoover worked for and with Bewick, Moreing until 1908, when he went off on his own. Further triumphs followed, so that by 1914 Hoover was recognized as a leading authority in the field not only of international mining, but international business. He was a businessman by then, and an empire builder in the mold of Carnegie, Hill, or Harriman. But there was a difference. The previous generation had been known for businessmen who attempted to carve empires for themselves, using large corporations as bases of operations. Hoover worked as head of a group of specialized engineers and technicians, which would take an interest in a mine in Burma, oil wells in Russia, copper mines in central Africa, and whatever else seemed profitable and worth the risks. "Our engineering practice extended over the United States, Canada, Mexico, Chile, Russia, Mongolia, Burma, Penang, New Zealand and Australia. The variety of our practice and their national settings gave infinite interests and in aggregate they paid us high fees."[17]

Hoover and men like him seemed the next logical step in the development of western capitalism. Expertness was their stock in trade; their bags were always packed. In 1910 alone he worked in America, England, Scotland,

France, Russia, Burma, Korea, and Japan. Hoover had offices in New York, San Francisco, London, Petrograd, and Paris. His personal worth was in excess of $4 million. He was only forty years old in 1914.

The Hoover Credo

Through all of this, Hoover remained intensely American, surprisingly parochial and withdrawn. He had not become sophisticated in the ways of the world. Indeed, all he saw, especially in the Orient and Europe, convinced him that America had little to learn from foreigners. In 1914 a friend wrote to him, asking for advice for a young man who wanted to pursue a career overseas. Hoover discouraged him. "The American is always an alien abroad," he wrote. "He can never assimilate. Nor do other peoples ever accept him otherwise than as a foreigner. His heart is in his own country."[18]

His travel and work led Hoover to believe in the innate superiority of whites over nonwhites, and of Americans over others of the western world (when Hoover spoke of Americans in this period, he meant whites only). As in most other things, Hoover judged by the result. In 1909, in a series of lectures on mining, he spoke of Asiatics and Negroes as "working labor of low mental order."

> In a general way, it may be stated with confidence that the white miners above mentioned can, under the same physical conditions, and with from five to ten times the wage, produce the same economic result—that is, an equal or lower cost per unit of production. Much observation and experience in working Asiatics and negroes as well as Americans and Australians in mines, lead the writer to the conclusion that, averaging actual results, one white man equals from two to three of the colored races, even in the simplest forms of mine work such as shoveling or tramming. In the most highly skilled branches, such as mechanics, the average ratio is as one to seven, or in extreme cases, even eleven.[19]

In other men this might be dismissed as racism, based perhaps on emotion, upbringing, or belief in some biological theory. This was not the case with Hoover. Neither in his writings, nor his public utterances later on, would he make statements that could be categorized as "racist" in the contexts of the times he lived in and the places he worked. Rather, it was simply the result of what he considered dispassionate observation. "The question is not entirely a comparison of bare efficiency individually," he wrote. "It is the sum total of results." "Americans must be careful not to get out of character with their essentially savage background or they will be misunderstood men," he wrote later on.[20]

Hoover respected the English, distrusted the French, and considered the Russians Asiatics, and therefore not really part of western civilization at all.[21] In one of the rare emotional statements in his *Memoirs* he wrote:

> In all my twenty years of professional "travelling" to and fro, I landed from ships onto American soil from abroad at least a hundred times. To me, every homecoming was an inspiration. I found always a more spontaneous kindliness, a great neighborliness, a greater sense of

individuality, a far deeper sense of equality, a lesser poverty, a greater comfort and security, and above all, a wider spread of education, a wider freedom of spirit and a wider confidence of every parent in the unlimited future of his children than in any other country in the world.

Europe, in contrast, offered "the explosive forces of nationalism, of imperialism, religious antagonism, age-old hates, memories of deep wrongs, revenges, fierce distrusts, repellent fears and dangerous poverty."[22]

The War Years

In early 1914 the Hoovers were more or less settled at Stanford, and with his enterprises in good shape, Hoover had time for various charities and public programs. He was asked to help in setting up an exposition and agreed to do so. In early March, as part of his contribution, he went to London to negotiate with the English regarding their contribution. While there, he expected to look over the work of his European operations.

Hoover was in London when World War I began. He immediately helped Americans stranded in Europe, which made him a minor public figure. Businessmen and politicians knew of Hoover before; now the general public began hearing his name. In October he was asked to take charge of Belgian relief assistance, establish programs to feed the hungry, and in general alleviate distress. Hoover accepted, and within a few months had become a world figure. He set up an administration, initiated contacts with major belligerents, obtained financial assistance from the powers, arranged purchasing agreements, and spoke to people on both sides over the heads of their elected officials. In other words, Hoover became the head of a state, complete in all regards except that of territoriality. He travelled from Paris to Berlin without being stopped by officials, was on good terms with Germans as well as French, and by 1917 wielded so much power that even Prime Minister Lloyd George was obliged to bow to his will when they clashed over the organization of Belgian relief.

The political leaders spoke to the peoples of their nations, or at best, their side in the war. Hoover was more than that; his constituency was international, and even nonnational. As the war progressed, the reputations of national leaders suffered, while Hoover's rose. In the process, the great engineer became the great humanitarian. Yet he was the same man, after all. In the past Hoover had regarded business as one way to help his fellow man—in the Rockefeller tradition, he had helped create jobs, produce goods, and distribute them, so as to raise standards of living. Now he was working to alleviate distress, offering charity to those who needed it, with the understanding it was a temporary measure, one that would last only so long as the people involved could not help themselves. He did his work efficiently, applying modern business techniques to humanitarian efforts in a way and on a scale never before achieved. "His one pursuit in life is getting things done—things that count," wrote Hugh Gibson, first secretary of the American legation in Brussels.

Efficiency receives his devoted service, but always with that discrimination that never loses sight of the human element of the people he is working for and those that are working with him. . . . He is modest to an extent that is sometimes painful to people who deal with him, and never suffers such acute misery as when being extolled publicly for what he has done. . . .[23]

Newspapers carried stories of Hoover's efforts, estimates of the number of people whose lives he saved, and predictions of his future in American life after the war. It seemed promising, to say the least.

The United States declared war in April, and in May President Wilson asked Hoover to join his administration as United States Food Administrator. He accepted, and so entered the federal bureaucracy. Now his mandate was not only to provide foodstuffs for the European allies, but to coordinate the procurement, supply, and distribution work in America, as well as conduct public relations for what amounted to a self-rationing program.

Hoover insisted on being in charge of his entire operation, and received Wilson's guarantees that such would be the case. A man who in the past had always been at the head of the organizational pyramid, Hoover did not work well as an underling, and always found it difficult to share responsibility and power. His relations with his staff was warm; Hoover rarely had problems dealing with subordinates. Nor did he clash often with other bureaucrats heading departments whose authority overlapped with his. In part this was because his reputation for efficiency, and his popularity, were such that few dared cross swords with him. There was also the matter of postwar planning, for in 1918 talk of Hoover's candidacy for the presidency in 1920—on either party ticket—was being seriously discussed in Washington.

Hoover's work at the Food Administration was hailed as a model of its kind; it was said he could squeeze more out of a dollar than any man in the capital. More important in terms of Hoover's development, however, was his study of the American economy and business practices, subjects of which he had known comparatively little at firsthand prior to accepting the assignment.

Hoover quickly realized that the economy was uncoordinated, that waste proliferated, and that federal power and suasion could be used to correct the problems. In 1917 there were 1,700 different types of wagon gears, 326 models of plows, and 784 agricultural drills and other planting machines. Hoover set about rationalizing these and related areas, so that by the end of the war the number of wheel sizes had been reduced to 4 and plows to 76. The development of interchangeable parts had begun a century before; with Hoover's help, it was speeded up considerably during the war.

Hoover did not attempt to order businessmen to rationalize. Instead, he relied upon their self-interest. As he saw it, the function of government was to show businessmen how they could best serve themselves, and how by so acting, they would benefit the nation. This could be done by bringing businessmen into the decision-making process and, to use a phrase later made famous, "help them help themselves." This system seemed to work. Writing of his experience later on, Hoover said:

About 95 percent of patriotic processors and distributors were controlled by the co-operating committees of the trades and by the regulations contracted with them. But it developed that there were about 5 percent who refused to join in our trade-committee agreements and sought to gain special advantages for themselves. In time, we were compelled to license several entire trades in order to circumvent these poachers. Reluctantly, we had to undertake the huge burden of issuing more than 250,000 licenses. During the period in which the licenses were in force, our Enforcement Division had about 8,000 cases of violations. Most of them were not willful, and our officials simply reminded the offenders of the law, and gave them a reprimand. In some cases of more gravity, we settled for a modest contribution to the Red Cross. . . . We actually cancelled only about 200 licenses out of 250,000, and those for willful or repeated violations. . . .[24]

Before the war some reformers, Wilson among them, seemed to believe that the government's function could be limited to that of a referee, which would make certain no single unit became so large and powerful as to destroy the others. The war ended this belief for most of them. A generation of businessmen and reformers went to Washington, participated in government and business-government relations, and derived lessons from that experience. For some businessmen and bureaucrats, the lesson was that unregulated capitalism might be outmoded. In the future, strong government participation in the economy might be needed. Some such individuals, among them Hugh Johnson, George Peek, Joseph Kennedy and, of course, Franklin Roosevelt, would apply this lesson during the New Deal. Another group, which included Hoover, agreed that unregulated competition was destructive, but believed that businessmen understood this, and with government aid—not control— self-regulation was possible. The associational movement appeared the best response to this situation, and Hoover and others like him came to lean heavily upon it. Such men like Ray Wilbur, Julius Barnes, Lewis Strauss, and Robert A. Taft worked with Hoover in this period, and came to the same conclusions. Their ideas would be reflected in the federal programs of the late 1920s and early 1930s; those of Roosevelt would be found in government in the 1930s, and more particularly, after 1935. After World War II, the struggle between the ideologies would continue, as it does to the present.

Hoover remained at his post after the war had ended, now using American food to feed European refugees and to help with rehabilitation work, but at the same time utilizing his power against what he believed to be a "wave of Bolshevism" sweeping in from Russia. American food was used to help overthrow a communist government in Hungary and install a reactionary anticommunist regime in that country. Finland's early flirtations with communism were ended by the power of American food shipments. At one time Hoover tried to turn the Versailles conference into an anticommunist coalition; he warned against a harsh peace for Germany, feeling that country would be needed to stem the advance of communism into central Europe. This was not a wholly popular idea at the time; Americans were anticommunist, to be sure, but they disliked the idea of assisting the hated Huns. Hoover was credited with humanitarian sentiments, however, and his popularity grew. This was not the first, nor would it be the last time his motives would be misunderstood. Even so astute an observer as John Maynard Keynes, then attached to the British delegation, thought Hoover wanted an easy peace because he recognized that the economic consequences of a harsh one could be international disaster. Writing at the time, he said:

> Mr. Hoover was the only man who emerged from the ordeal of Paris with an enhanced reputation. This complex personality, with his habitual air of weary Titan (or, as others might put it, of exhausted prize fighter), his eyes steadily fixed on the true and essential facts of the European situation, imported into the Councils of Paris, when he took part in them, precisely that atmosphere of reality, knowledge, magnanimity and disinterestedness which, if they had been found in other quarters, also, would have given us the Good Peace.[25]

As early as 1919, Frank Cobb of the New York *World* had supported Hoover for the Republican presidential nomination. Now the powerful *Saturday Evening Post* joined in, and was followed by other journals (Document 1). Hoover was a nominal Republican, but his allegiance to the GOP was shaky. In 1912 he had backed the bolting Theodore Roosevelt's run on the Progressive ticket, and had made a small donation to his campaign. But this had little significance since Hoover was unconcerned with politics prior to the war. Also, some Democrats, among them Louis B. Wehle, a Wilson appointee, noted that Hoover had worked well in a Democratic administration, backed the League of Nations, and showed signs of interest in that party's nomination. Wehle had a "dream ticket"—Hoover for president, Franklin D. Roosevelt for vice-president. Roosevelt spoke to Hoover of the possibility, but received no encouragement. By early 1920, it was clear that Hoover was a Republican. It was also obvious that the party had no intention of offering him its nomination.[26]

In the Cabinet

In the end party professionals selected Harding, who went on to defeat Democrat James Cox in the general election. Soon afterwards, Harding asked Hoover to join his cabinet as secretary of commerce. For the next eight years Hoover would occupy that office, using it not only to put his ideas into practice, but to outline them for the American people.

In 1922 Hoover wrote a short book entitled *American Individualism*, in which he set down his creed. It contained no new idea, original statement, or bold approach to problems. Nor did it show a novel insight into the American experience. Instead, it was an amalgam of Social Darwinsim, anticommunism, patriotism, and the associational ideal. Hoover considered one paragraph important, and he italicized it in the text. Yet it was the kind of material Americans had heard for years.

> Therefore, it is not the individualism of other countries for which I would speak, but the individualism of America. Our individualism differs from all others because it embraces these great ideals: *that while we build our society upon the attainment of the individual, we shall safeguard to every individual an equality of opportunity to take that*

position in the community to which his intelligence, character, ability, and ambition entitle him; that we keep the social solution free from the frozen state of classes; that we shall stimulate effort of each individual to achievement; that through an enlarging sense of responsibility and understanding we shall assist him to this attainment while he in turn must stand up to the emery wheel of competition.[27]

One of the stories told of Hoover in this period was that while walking in Washington, he was stopped by a beggar who asked him for a coin. Hoover talked to the man for a moment, but gave him nothing. The following day the beggar was approached by one of Hoover's aides, who offered him a job. The story may not have been true, but it was the kind American businessmen, raised in the 1890s and functioning in the 1920s, would appreciate. The same was true for *American Individualism.* It was the credo of the past, with few additions or attempts to adjust it to the realities of the present. Hoover's anticommunism added a contemporary flavor, and his engineering background made it appear "modern." In speaking out as he did, Hoover seemed to combine the old-fashioned virtues of a Calvin Coolidge with the new technology as symbolized by a Charles Lindbergh. He was new, he was modern, he was up-to-date, while at the same time he retained all the basic beliefs of the late nineteenth century. Little wonder, then, that Hoover— despite his lack of personal magnetism and inability to inspire any except close associates—became so popular in the 1920s.

On taking office, Hoover was told by a previous secretary of commerce that the job would present few difficulties. All you have to do, he said, is to make certain the fish were to bed and the lighthouses turned on at each coast. This was generally true; in the past, the Commerce Department had had little impact. Hoover changed this, using his position to provide leadership and guidance for business. In addition, he continually intruded upon the work of other department heads, especially State, Labor, and Agriculture. It was said that Hoover was secretary of commerce, and assistant secretary of everything else.

But Hoover did not oblige businessmen to do anything they themselves thought undesirable. Speaking before the National Association of Manufacturers in 1922, he said, "Now all of these services are purely voluntary relationships with industry and commerce. There is no regulatory function in the Department of Commerce, minus a few inconsequential matters in connection with the safety of human life, and it is my feeling that in order that this Department shall be of the greatest service to commerce and industry, it should be maintained on a non-regulatory basis [applause], that its whole relationship should be one of cooperation with our business public. . . ."[28]

Business would be helped by government, but not regulated. And all could become businessmen, if they but submitted to the "emery wheel of competition." "In America we want to go ahead," he said in 1924. "Just where do we want to go? As I see it, we want to get greater security in living, greater education, greater social and political justice, greater moral fiber—*for everybody who will work, and for nobody else.*"[29] This too, was applauded (Document 2).

This did not mean Hoover opposed the lower class; indeed, throughout the 1920s he applauded workers "who wanted to work," and were ambitious. Increased business efficiency and the application of the latest technology to industry would enable wages to rise, providing a higher standard of living for all. The American Federation of Labor, a moderate organization in the 1920s, was still viewed with a jaundiced eye by many old-line businessmen, but not by Hoover, who applauded organization and association among workers as he did among businessmen. "It is my opinion that our nation is very fortunate in having the American Federation of Labor," he said, and in 1928 his presidential candidacy was supported by John L. Lewis of the United Mine Workers, Matthew Woll of the Photoengravers, and William Hutcheson of the United Brotherhood of Carpenters and Joiners, one of the most powerful men in the labor movement, while A.F. of L. President William Green, though neutral, made pro-Hoover statements. Business, which by then had come to wholeheartedly accept the associational idea, also gave Hoover strong support and its cheers when he said:

> We are passing from a period of excessively individualistic action into a period of associational activities in business. . . . I think we are in the presence of a new era in the organization of industry and commerce pregnant with infinite possibilities of moral progress. . . . We have perhaps twenty-five thousand associational activities in the American economic field. The membership of the associations conducting these activities must be open to all participants in the industry or trade, or else rival organizations come into existence at once. . . . The total interdependence of all industries compels trade associations in the long run to go parallel to the general economic good. . . . I believe that through these forces we are slowly moving toward some sort of industrial democracy. . . . With these private collective agencies used as the machinery for the elimination of abuses and the cultivation of high standards, I am convinced that we shall have entered a great new era of self-governing industry.[30]

So the candidate of labor and management, uniting both with his old-fashioned philosophy of work, his belief in cooperation rather than conflict, and his strong record both in private and public life, won the election of 1928 (Documents 3-a and 3-b). No other man seemed as capable of handling the presidency than did Hoover in 1928. Not even Coolidge, who by then was being compared with Abraham Lincoln, had his reputation. The shrewd Coolidge realized this; his time had passed. He was good at saving money and keeping the waters calm, he told a friend. Perhaps the time was ripe for a man who spent money and promoted change.

In his State of the Union message of December 4, 1928, Coolidge said "No Congress of the United States ever assembled, on surveying the state of the Union, has met with a more pleasing domestic prospect than that which appears at the present time. In the domestic field there is tranquility and contentment. . . ."[31] Three months later, Hoover echoed the sentiment in his Inaugural Address:

> Ours is a land rich in resources; stimulating in its glorious beauty; filled with millions of happy homes; blessed with comfort and opportunity. In no nation are the institutions of progress more advanced. In no

nation are the fruits of accomplishment more secure. In no nation is the government more worthy of respect. No country is more loved by its people. I have an abiding faith in their capacity, integrity and high purpose. I have no fears for the future of our country. It is bright with hope (*Alternative* 4: see Document 4).[32]

Notes

1. *Time*, March 26, 1928, p. 9.

2. Samuel Crowther, *The Presidency Vs. Hoover* (Garden City: Doubleday-Page and Co., 1928), p. 57. Also see Will Irwin, *Herbert Hoover: A Reminiscent Biography* (New York: Houghton, Mifflin and Co., 1928), which became the semiofficial campaign biography of the candidate. Irwin had been a schoolmate of Hoover's at Stanford, and in 1928 was a well-known journalist. William Hard, *Who's Hoover?* (New York: Dodd, Mead, and Co., 1928), also praised Hoover, but as the title indicated, raised questions about him that Hard felt needed answers. It was written more in the spirit of the *Time* article than the other books, and was one of the best attempts at psycho-biography ever published. Later on, it would be used as ammunition in the anti-Hoover campaign of 1932. By then, Hard's own questions had become public ones, and Hard abandoned Hoover to support Franklin Roosevelt.

3. Many of the early presidents were businessmen in the sense they speculated in land and ran plantations. But they did not consider themselves as such, and in any case lacked the modern capitalist outlook.

4. Interestingly enough, the next president to be charged by some as being rootless was Richard Nixon who, like Hoover, was a Quaker and who spent formative years in California. The two men share other characteristics, and their personalities appear somewhat similar.

5. There are thousands of pictures of Hoover, and almost all seem to indicate that he hated to have his picture taken. From these he appeared stiff, unsmiling, and rather forbidding. Cameramen did manage to get some posed shots of Hoover while fishing, and some of these show a happy, relaxed, convivial man.

6. Irwin Hood (Ike) Hoover, *Forty-Two Years in the White House* (New York: Houghton Mifflin Co., 1934), p. 87.

7. In 1928 Hoover told a journalist that he enjoyed food. " 'You see,' he said simply, 'I was always hungry then.' " Ray T. Tucker, "Is Hoover Human?" *North American Review* 226, no. 5 (November, 1928): 513. The article's title is interesting. One would hardly have asked such a question of any other presidential candidate.

8. This is not to say Hoover did not have an intellectual side. Together with his wife, he translated Agricola's *De Re Metallica* from Latin to English in 1909.

9. Herbert Hoover, *The Memoirs of Herbert Hoover: Years of Adventure, 1874-1920* (New York: Macmillan, 1951), p. 1. Hoover's talk of his youth reminds one of the ending of *Citizen Kane*, the Orson Welles motion picture, in which Charles Kane, the wealthy publisher, thinks of "Rosebud," his childhood sled, just before he died. Kane was supposedly modelled after William Randolph Hearst, but there were some elements of Hoover there too and, for that matter, of many prominent men of that generation.

10. Clement Wood, *Herbert Clark Hoover: An American Tragedy* (New York: Swain, 1932), p. 15.

11. Hard, *Who's Hoover?*, pp. 41-42, 52.

12. "Hoover's mind is not—in the ordinary sense of the word—an 'artistic' mind. It is indeed a highly cultivated mind. It perceives—that is—the speculations of life as well as its activities, its calls to understanding as well as its calls to action. Few men have a greater refinement of mind than Hoover. His route to it, however, is not through the arts. It is through the sciences. It is on avenues along which words are laggards." Hard, *Who's Hoover?*, p. 50.

13. In 1931, Hoover said, "Ninety percent of our problems are caused by fear." Two years later, Franklin D. Roosevelt proclaimed, " . . . the only thing we have to fear is

fear itself—nameless, unreasoning, unjustified terror which paralyzes needed effort to convert retreat into advance." The difference between these two statements is that between science and art—the ability to inform and the will to inspire, an appeal to the brain and one to the heart. Needless to say, Roosevelt's statement is famous, while Hoover's is forgotten today.

14. Twenty years later Hoover wrote of what he considered the best kind of education for young people. He recommended science and engineering, because "that sort of exactness makes for truth and conscience." Science was worthy even for those who had no desire to become scientists. "It might be good for the world if more men had that sort of mental start in life, even if they did not pursue the profession." *Memoirs: Years of Adventure*, p. 132.

15. Ibid., pp. 19-20.

16. Hoover's first impression of London is worth noting. "I have ever since envied other Americans their first visit to England. Familiarity wears off the vivid stimulation of personal discovery of the great monuments of history, but in time the comparative poverty and the servility of the mass of people to class distinction brings disillusionment." The theme recurred throughout Hoover's life. The more he travelled, the more American he felt. Ibid., pp. 29-30.

17. Ibid., pp. 115-16.

18. Hard, *Who's Hoover?*, pp. 65-66.

19. Herbert C. Hoover, *Principles of Mining* (New York: McGraw-Hill, 1909), p. 163.

20. Hoover, *Memoirs: Years of Adventure*, p. 97.

21. Hoover's experience in Russia began in the eastern part of the then-empire, among the Mongols. In 1923, when he helped end the famine in Russia, he received a message from some of the people who had worked a mine of his, "saying they would be 'good and obedient' if we would only give them work again." Hoover hated communism not only because he felt it was inimical to everything worthwhile in life, but also because it represented the intrusion of an oriental despotism into western culture, Ibid., p. 106.

22. Ibid., pp. 123-24.

23. Hugh Gibson, "Herbert C. Hoover," *Century* 94, no. 3 (August, 1917): 517.

24. Herbert C. Hoover, *An American Epic* (Chicago: H. Regnery and Co., 1960), Vol. 2, pp. 55-56.

25. John Maynard Keynes, *The Economic Consequences of The Peace* (New York: Harcourt, Brace and Howe, 1919), p. 257.

26. Hoover did run in the California primary, opposing Senator Hiram Johnson, who had been Teddy Roosevelt's vice-presidential running mate in 1912. Without campaigning, he received 210,000 votes to Johnson's 370,000, an impressive showing. Johnson and other reform Republicans never forgave him this action.

27. Herbert C. Hoover, *American Individualism* (Garden City: Doubleday, Page and Co., 1922), pp. 9-10.

28. James W. Prothro, *The Dollar Decade: Business Ideas in the 1920s* (Baton Rouge: Louisiana State University Press, 1954), p. 140.

29. Hard, *Who's Hoover?*, p. 14.

30. Ibid., p. 255.

31. New York *Times*, December 5, 1928.

32. New York *Times*, March 5, 1929.

3

The Atmosphere of '29

Americans celebrate the coming and going of their presidents in much the same fashion as the English used to do for their monarchs. The assumption is made that the new man—especially if he replaces a person of the opposite political party—will set the nation on a new course, or at least significantly alter the old. Perhaps reflecting the vestiges of the campaign, his supporters speak as though the problems of the past will finally be met and resolved, while his opponents, leaving power, see their programs and dreams on the way to the scrap heap, with disaster waiting around the bend.

The inauguration of Jefferson was viewed by Federalists as the beginning of the end for the national government, a signal for the importation of radicalism to Washington. John Quincy Adams saw in Andrew Jackson's 1828 victory anarchy and rebellion in power. The coming of Lincoln signalled an end to the value of union for a significant group of southerners. In recent times the inaugurations of Kennedy and Nixon were described as major turning points in American history.

New presidents often encourage such beliefs. For example, in his 1961 Inaugural Address, Kennedy said, "Let the word go forth from this time and place, to friend and foe alike, that the torch has been passed to a new generation of Americans . . . " In fact, new administrations, even new generations, rarely can "turn the nation around." Seldom in American history has a new president been able significantly to reverse the policies of his predecessor soon after taking office. Few have even tried to do so, and most of those who did failed.

There are several reasons for this. In the first place, Americans have never elected a truly radical candidate to the presidency. In practice, all but a few have stressed continuity rather than change, although their rhetoric might have led some to believe otherwise. Indeed, most presidents—Jefferson and Lincoln among them—have attempted to heal the wounds of the campaign on entering the White House, assuring foes they had little to fear from the new administration. Even those who wanted to initiate change found it difficult to do so. Much of the old bureaucracy continued in office, doing the same things the same way, with little heed as to who was president or what he wanted done. Congress and the Supreme Court would also check the president or attempt to push him into ways other than those he might want to travel. The national government was established in such a way as to discourage major shifts in programs, to cripple ambitious plans, to hinder the efforts of most strong presidents assuming office, and to cow the weak into submission. This is not to say that presidents do not institute major changes, or on occasion achieve great power.

36

Rather, the occasions are few, and rarely do they come at the beginning of the administration, when followers and foes most expect to see them. It is then that the form of power, the style, the appearance may appear different, while the content is often the same as that of the immediate past.

The Hoover State

Hoover could not have changed the Coolidge policies even had he so desired. His predecessor was extremely popular at the time he left office; Coolidge could have won renomination in 1928 and then gone on to a great victory over anyone the Democrats might have named. Hoover knew this, and in his Inaugural Address departed from tradition to speak of his predecessor by name. "For wise guidance in this great period of recovery the Nation is deeply indebted to Calvin Coolidge (Document 4)." In his first months in office, Hoover did little to depart from the Coolidge programs or to change the direction in which the country had been led.

But there were changes in form and style. Some of these were minor, the kind newspaper columnists loved to write about, but which had little lasting importance. Since Hoover's reputation had been that of an engineer and technician, the most frequently used adjectives those first months were "efficient" and "modern." For example, Hoover had a telephone installed at his desk; he was the first president to do so. His predecessors all made do with one secretary; Hoover had five, each with specific duties, and he kept them all "hopping." The presidential yacht *Olympia* was retired, for a savings of around $300,000. The White House stables were closed down, cutting $15,000 a year from the budget. Hoover seemed to be everywhere, urging efficiency on his staff, cutting expenses wherever he could, always on the go, never relaxing. He seemed as activist a president as Theodore Roosevelt, but where Roosevelt exuded glamour and "vigor," Hoover's moves were purposeful and well-directed. Results, not image, seemed the order of the day during the first part of the Hoover administration. But in the process, an image of efficiency, intelligence, and knowledge was created. The "modern presidency," the right kind of man for the New Era, seemed in the process of creation.

Even Hoover's recreation appeared purposeful. He formed the "medicine ball cabinet," consisting of cabinet members, some Supreme Court justices, and a few select newspapermen, who would get together with the president before breakfast and throw a heavy medicine ball to one another. Through such exercise Hoover attempted to keep fit, after ballooning to well over two hundred pounds in his last days in the Coolidge cabinet. It was quite different from Roosevelt's hunting trips, where competition was sought after and victory the prize. Medicine ball had only one purpose: health. It contained no element of sport or competition, but rather consisted of a group of middle-aged men trying to retain their vigor for hard tasks ahead. The difference between Rooseveltian and Hooverian sports was lost on the press, however. The meetings were well-publicized, and contrasted favorably with

Coolidge's long afternoon naps and Harding's activities with the "poker cabinet," which would meet regularly to play cards, drink booze, smoke cigars, and tell racy tales. Hoover had "associates," not cronies, in his recreation, and this too was a change. Harding had been loved for his humanity, and Coolidge received affection for his dry wit, cracker-barrel approach to government, and apparent simplicity. Hoover did not inspire love or affection. He was admired; the public stood in awe of him those first months in the White House. Much had been written of the "new man" being created in the Soviet Union, a man who would "fit" the requirements of the new civilization the Russians were attempting to construct. America too was building a new civilization, or so it seemed at the time. And Hoover was the American version of the new man. But something was lost, too. Hoover evoked respect, not love and affection, and of the three, respect is the least permanent sentiment.

Almost every new president undergoes a short "honeymoon" period after his inauguration, and Hoover's lasted longer than most. Within a few weeks, however, criticisms of some of his activities were heard. Hoover seemed intent on controlling every aspect of the executive branch. His cabinet was considered one of the least distinguished in years, in large part due to the President's desire to dictate policy. Andrew Mellon remained at Treasury and Henry Stimson, who had been secretary of war in the Taft Cabinet and later on had a distinguished diplomatic career, went to State. The others, however, were deemed mediocre, servile, or inconsequential. Secretary of War James Good had served in the House from 1909 to 1921 with little distinction, and then had returned to practice law in Illinois, taking time out to serve as western campaign manager for Coolidge in 1924. Secretary of the Interior Ray Wilbur and Secretary of Agriculture Arthur Hyde were able men, but would not have been selected for their posts were it not for their long friendships with the president. Secretary of Commerce Robert Lamont, who took Hoover's old job, had worked with the president during World War I, had been open in his admiration for Hoover ideas, and was devoted to "the Chief." The others followed the same pattern. Such men would carry out plans, not institute them. They didn't complain when Hoover ended the practice of allowing cabinet members to name their own assistants, dictating the selection from the White House. There were no independent figures in the administration, as had been the case in previous ones. Harding had selected Mellon, Charles Evans Hughes, and Hoover himself for his cabinet, although all three had national reputations and at times overshadowed the president himself. Coolidge had kept them on, and even put up with Secretary of Agriculture Henry C. Wallace, whose ideas were almost diametrically opposite to his own.

No one would be permitted such freedom in the Hoover administration, which was noteworthy for its homogeneity. Hoover must have thought it made sense; after all, no business could be run with different camps going in different directions. To some newspapermen, however, it appeared the new president was power hungry, determined to crush all opposition and abolish free discussion and debate within his official family.

The newspapermen themselves had difficulties with Hoover. In the first place, the president was notoriously thin-skinned, and agonized over criticism of his policies and behavior. Once, while secretary of commerce, he complained to Coolidge about a story he had read in one paper. Coolidge laconically answered, "I never bother reading articles that displease me." Of course this was not so, and was another example of Coolidge's brand of humor. In fact, most politicians attempt to maintain cordial if not friendly relations with the press, realizing that newspapermen may be used to serve their interests. Although he had a reputation for rarely speaking, and never using two words when one would suffice, Coolidge provided the newspapermen with good copy. At his press conferences, he would respond to questions submitted earlier in the week; and was often lively and witty. When on vacation Coolidge would fraternize with reporters, and in fact was quite popular with the Washington press corps. The newsmen, in turn, helped Coolidge preserve his image of homespun simplicity. A shrewd politician and in his own way a sophisticated leader, Coolidge enjoyed playing the country bumpkin on occasion. Vermont farmers knew what he was doing, even though New York intellectuals were completely taken in. Coolidge did not give the appearance of minding criticism from the press, accepted it with grace, never retaliated against a reporter, and never played favorites. In this way he earned the affection and respect of the Washington newsmen, which in turn helped prevent future negative stories from being filed. It was good politics, and Coolidge was always a good politician.

Either Hoover did not understand the great game of politics or refused to play. Still the businessman in politics, he viewed the press as an adversary. He held this feeling on entering the White House in triumph, and it would grow as his difficulties mounted and press criticism followed. Rarely would Hoover allow the photographers to take pictures of him—he felt they made him appear weak and flabby—and on several occasions he fled from photographers or ordered them from his office. His secretaries reflected his views on the press, and one of them, George Akerson, barely disguised his contempt for reporters. Within weeks the press corps dubbed the secretaries the "vestal virgins," since they seemed to serve the president without question or thought of their own, existing as his mouthpiece, like mechanical men.

Like all presidents, Hoover planted stories with newsmen, almost always through the secretaries. Coolidge had done the same. But when Coolidge had been discovered, the newspapermen considered it part of the game. The president had won this round; they would win the next. Hoover had a different view of the situation. When reporters uncovered the plants and printed them as such, Hoover would become furious, and later snub the reporters involved. In other words, he would not play the game according to the rules, either because he did not know the rules, or was emotionally unable to accept them.

In addition, Hoover played favorites. He was especially fond of Mark Sullivan of the New York *Herald Tribune*, a member of the medicine-ball cabinet along with a handful of reporters. After their exercise, the men would gather for coffee and toast. Then most would leave—while Hoover, Sullivan, and a few close friends, but no other reporters, would remain for the regular breakfast. As a result, Sullivan's articles on administration happenings were the most accurate to be had. A wise and experienced reporter, as well as one in tune with Hoover's basic philosophy, Sullivan continued to maintain his close relations with the president throughout his administration. Meanwhile other reporters—especially those who wrote for newspapers owned by Democrats, or which had supported Smith in the bitter 1928 campaign—were ignored. Even Richard Oulahan of the New York *Times*, an urbane and sophisticated reporter who was on good terms with Hoover and thought along similar lines as the president, showed displeasure with favoritism. By late summer of 1929, Hoover was as popular with the country as he had ever been, but his relations with the press were poor.[1] The same people who might have commiserated with a Harding or have been manipulated by Coolidge, were prepared and in some cases eager to pounce on Hoover's mistakes and difficulties.

The Political Context

All presidents from Theodore Roosevelt to Coolidge had strained relations with Congress at one time or another. Prior to the war the reform impulse had resulted in a tripartite division in the legislature, with one group insisting on the maintenance of the status quo, another attempting to pass sweeping reform measures, and a third willing to accept half a loaf in such matters. Roosevelt had been a master of Congress, alternatively bullying it, ignoring it, using public opinion to obtain passage of reform measures, and making modest changes appear drastic and vice versa. Taft's inability to deal effectively with Congress was a major reason for his failures, while Wilson's battles with the Senate over the League of Nations were famous. Harding was respectful of the Republican senatorial caucus at first and often did its bidding, though toward the end of his administration he had begun to show independence. Congress was wary of Coolidge; he generally had poor relations with all three factions, but escaped conflict by asking for little in the way of legislation. Instead, he would frustrate congressional action through vetoes, relying upon public good will for support. Most of the time he was successful and prevailed. Congress could damage the ambitions of an activist president; an inactive one had little trouble besting the legislature, especially one with the political skills of a Coolidge.

It was obvious from the first that Hoover intended to be an activist. He called Congress into special session on April 15 to discuss agricultural and tariff policies, and hopefully to pass new legislation in these areas (*Alternative 5:* see Document 5). The Republicans were in firm control of both chambers, with margins of 254 to 143 in the House and 56 to 39 in the Senate. This was deceptive. In fact, there were strong anti-Hoover elements in the legislature, and by the end of the special session, the president had lost whatever control of Congress he had on Inauguration Day.

There were several reasons for Hoover's failures on Capitol Hill. First, he "and his kind" were disliked by the Republican professionals in Congress. Even though Hoover had been in government since 1917, he remained very much the outsider. Hoover had few close acquaintances in Congress; as secretary of commerce he had been aloof and distant, and showed little sympathy for the give-and-take of the political arena. If the policy were good, it should be put into effect, he thought. Politics, compromise, wheeling-and-dealing, should not enter into consideration. But it did on Capitol Hill, and although Hoover recognized the fact, he dealt with it clumsily. Harding, himself a creature of both the Congress and machine politics, had been able to work in harmony both with the legislature and state and local politicians, dispensing patronage in a way that if not wise, was well done. Coolidge also understood and accepted the political facts of life, and if not loved, was at least accepted as one of their own kind by the GOP politicos. Hoover lacked Coolidge's sophistication and Harding's ability to please. Even after receiving the Republican presidential nomination, he maintained his distance from the established politicians within the party. Instead, he surrounded himself with his own men, usually people without an independent base of power of their own, who called Hoover "the Chief." Such was the way in a large business enterprise, and Hoover meant to practice such policies within the party. Needless to say, the Republican professionals never came to terms with such an idea. Afterwards, when Hoover relented and began to dispense patronage through the local GOP clubs, he did so in a clumsy fashion that brought criticism from the press and the Democrats and embarassment to Republican leaders, both within Congress and on the state and local level. Not until after he left the White House would Hoover be embraced by the party, and even then not all Republicans considered him "one of theirs."

In several matters, the tariff and agricultural policies included, Hoover attempted to instruct and educate legislators, who resented his presumptuousness (Document 5). The new president lacked a feel for the politics of sensitive legislation and did not understand that at times legislators have to consider the feelings of their constituents and special interests rather than what Hoover liked to call "the good of the country." Nor could he accept the long-standing tension that had existed between Congress and the White House, a conflict most professionals recognized as not a personal clash, but an institutional one, necessary in a representative republic. Hoover often neglected to perform the little acts of courtesy and ritualistic deference from one branch to another which on the surface may have seemed senseless, but in practice provided some of the grease that enabled the machinery of government to operate. He would announce appointments to minor posts rather than allowing congressmen to do so. He spoke to local leaders without informing representatives and senators of the fact. Even when dedicating public buildings he at times neglected to include local party leaders. Were it not for some fast work by his secretaries, the situation might have been worse than it was. Even then, Hoover's disdain of such matters was common knowledge in Washington, and did him grave harm when good will was needed later.

The Republican "establishment" in Congress was led by Senator George Moses of New Hampshire, the president pro tem, who had been in the Senate since 1918 and in politics since 1889. Senate majority floor leader James E. Watson of Indiana had entered the House in 1895 and the Senate in 1920. Senate whip Simeon Fess of Ohio was elected to the House in 1912 and moved up to the Senate in 1923. Reed Smoot of Utah, the acknowledged leader of Republican conservatives, a man who had worked well with Harding and Coolidge and provided votes to sustain vetoes of reform legislation, had a long-standing feud with Hoover, going back to the time they had served together on the World War Foreign Debt Commission in 1922. These men and other "old guard" Republicans, men who came up under William McKinley, accepted Theodore Roosevelt, and admired Coolidge's policies, had little in common with Hoover. On his part, the new president did not go out of his way to ingratiate himself with them. When he needed their help, it was not forthcoming.

Nor could Hoover rely upon his party's progressive wing. Some of its members had rallied behind Robert LaFollette and then gone on to leave the GOP and join Theodore Roosevelt's Progressive party in 1912. They returned later, but the split between the old guard and former progressives did not heal, and in 1924 a number of the latter group again rejected the Republican nominee, this time Coolidge, to back LaFollette's new Progressive party. One of their number, George Norris of Nebraska, had supported Al Smith against Hoover in 1928, going so far as to deliver radio speeches for the Democrat.

"Fighting Bob" LaFollette was dead in 1929, and had been succeeded by his son, "Young Bob." William Borah of Idaho, Norris, Hiram Johnson of California, Peter Norbeck of South Dakota, Smith Brookhart of Iowa, and Henrik Shipstead of Minnesota were considered members of the insurgent Republican group, which though poorly organized and led, represented a sizeable bloc in the Senate. Called the "Sons of the Wild Jackass" by their opponents, they liked to think of themselves as independents and reformers.[3] But they had no agenda for reform, and their individualism prevented organization for specific sets of goals. For the most part, they were isolationists, in favor of federal aid for farmers, and against a high tariff. The old guard, for its part, opposed federal assistance and supported proposals for higher duties on imports. Hoover was distrusted by the old guard. His work under Harding and Coolidge earned him the emnity of the insurgents, who also disliked his support for the League of Nations and identification as an internationalist. The president opposed the progressive plans for farm support, but not as strongly as the regulars would have preferred. He spoke of a "scientific tariff," and in a way that alienated members of both camps.

The old guard and the insurgent progressive Republicans offered alternatives to the Hoover approach. Both had been derived from the experiences, emotions, and dogmas of pre-World War I America. The "young Turks" of 1912 were old men by 1929, their most effective leader in the grave and no new one on the scene to take his place. The old guard was just that—old, and guarding a world that had begun to fade when McKinley was assassinated, and that received its death blow during the Great War. Hoover represented a new Republican approach, one that retained elements held dear by both factions, embellished with the aura of scientism. The alternative was there to be "sold" to the two factions; perhaps a better politician than Hoover, given time, could have accomplished the task, and in the process not only united the party, but set it on a new direction. Hoover lacked the political acumen and time needed for the job.

The Republicans in Congress were divided in 1929, as they had been for more than a generation. But they were together in opposing Hoover. He was unacceptable to the insurgents and distrusted by the regulars. The former considered him a spokesman for business, while the latter saw in him a disruptive influence, an amateur in politics, and a threat to their power in his independent base of support among businessmen and his smashing victory at the polls. On different occasions both wings would attack him; at no time did he lead a united party, win the confidence of more than a small minority of his party's political professionals, or create a significant "Hoover constituency" on Capitol Hill. In this respect, Hoover proved the most inept presidential leader of his own forces since Taft.

The Democratic Opposition

Hoover's relations with the Democrats were somewhat more complex. The Democratic divisions of 1924, between the William Gibbs McAdoo southern based prohibitionists and old Wilsonians with their overlay of anti-Catholicism and ties to the Ku Klux Klan, and the Al Smith northern urban antiprohibitionists, Catholic, facing other problems than those considered important by the Wilsonians, remained in 1928. Because of this Hoover had done well in the South, and a large contingent of southern Democrats was sympathetic to him. They thought Hoover had defeated Smith and so saved the country and cleansed the Democratic party. He would do nothing on the prohibition front, they believed. And he promised some kind of aid for agriculture. An astute politician might have cultivated them. Hoover did not, and by 1930 the southern Democrats were in opposition to him.

Reform Democrats of the Wilsonian stripe opposed big business, even more so than the insurgent Republicans. Hoover's identification with large corporations, and his probusiness stands as secretary of commerce alienated them. Senate floor leader Joseph T. Robinson of Arkansas and his assistant, Thomas J. Walsh of Montana, had no affection for the new president. Key Pittman of Nevada, the Democratic whip, believed him to be a symbol of eastern forces out to crush the West. By 1930 these three were able to unite most of the senate Democrats against the administration. But like the congressional Republicans, they could offer no cohesive alternative to the Hoover policies. The Democrats spent more time arguing the virtues of prohibition and recalling the divisions between the urban and rural, northern and southern wings of the party, than in mounting a concerted attack against Hoover's policies, or developing a critique of the associational approach.

Finally, there was the Democratic Party leadership, firmly in the hands of John J. Raskob, the multimillionaire businessman who had deserted the GOP to aid in the campaign of his coreligionist, Al Smith. Raskob had been unused to the hurley-burley of politics, and had been deeply stung by the anti-Catholicism of some of the Republican workers. As any businessman might, he blamed it on the candidate, Hoover, even though other Democrats told him that Hoover had nothing to do with the smears. Now he vowed revenge. Raskob stayed on as national chairman after Smith's defeat, and set about organizing the party for opposition to Hoover and, hopefully, a rematch in 1932. Jouett Shouse, a former Kansas congressman, a businessman who had also served as assistant secretary of the treasury under Wilson, and a most astute politician, remained as permanent paid director of the party, and was told to initiate an anti-Hoover program designed to destroy the president's reputation. Raskob and Shouse hired Charles Michelson, a veteran reporter who had been head of the Washington bureau for the New York *World*, as publicity agent. Michelson knew the capital better than most newsmen, and like a majority of them, disliked Hoover. He accepted the post readily, and began organizing for the anti-Hoover campaign, that hopefully would end with a renomination of Smith and a replay of 1928.[4]

The Democratic leadership, then, offered little in the way of an alternative to Hoover in 1929. Prohibition and revenge, not a response to the associational ideal, were discussed at party headquarters.

These were the forces and men Hoover faced on coming to office on March 4. They reflected old and often outworn ideas, and had less understanding of the nature of the economy than did the president. They would oppose him out of partisan sentiment or in the name of old institutions and crusades. The Republicans did not support Hoover as a man or an ideologist, even while they recognized and respected his political power and popularity. The Democrats, unruly and in disarray, could do little against him at the time. The opposition party would not receive leadership and a new rationale until the nomination of Franklin Roosevelt in 1932, and then he would either sweep out the old leaders or ignore them. But in 1929 Roosevelt was only governor of New York, a potential presidential candidate to be sure, but one far from power either in Washington or at Democratic headquarters. The alternative to the associational idea was in the wings, but would not emerge during the first years of the Hoover administration.

On April 16, 1929, with scarcely sufficient time to organize his administration, initiate relations with other branches of government, and survey the political scene, Hoover addressed a special session of Congress. "I have called this special session of Congress to redeem two pledges given in the last election—farm relief and limited changes in the tariff," he began (Document 5). Next to prohibition itself, agriculture was the most thorny issue of both the 1924 and 1928 elections, while the tariff was closely connected with it. Now Hoover would attempt to solve both, and in the process help pass the first piece of major legislation embodying the associational ideology with which he had become identified. He would demonstrate how scientific business practice could cut through old political knots, and in the process set the tone for his administration as well as point its direction.

The Farm Dilemma

Agriculture was the weakest sector of the economy during the boom years of the 1920s. Some of the farmers' problems resulted from the growth of industrialization and urbanization. The 1920 census reported that for the first time, more Americans were living in cities and large towns than in the countryside. Throughout the nineteenth century farm acreage had increased steadily, in both good years and bad; some 13 million acres were abandoned in the 1919-1924 period. In 1919 farmers had received sixteen percent of the national income; in 1929 the figure was nine percent. By almost any set of objective statistics, farming would appear to be a declining industry in the 1920s.

Some of the farmers' difficulties were man-made. During the war period of 1914-1918 farmers had been encouraged to expand their operations, and so they did, sinking in debt to provide food for the Allies as well as for Americans. The end of the war changed this, while "normalcy" meant farmers were left with overdeveloped acreage, large debts, declining markets, and little political leverage with business-oriented administrations. The high tariffs of the 1920s hurt farmers by enabling American manufacturers to raise prices higher than might otherwise have been the case, while at the same time making the farmers compete in the world market, where the price-setting mechanism operated to their disadvantage. The lower prices fell, the more American farmers attempted to produce, in order to keep their incomes on an even keel. This in turn led to still lower prices, and the process then repeated itself. The only way out of this spiral and the farmers' difficulties, thought the powerful Farm Bureau Federation, was through federal assistance.

The upshot was the creation of a "farm bloc," consisting of southern and midwestern legislators, leaders of farmer associations, and paid lobbyists. It was a political association, formed for political purposes. And it was effective. In 1921 it helped pass the Packers and Stockyards Act and the Grain Futures Act, which protected farmers against grain dealers, while the Capper-Volstead Act of 1922 exempted farm marketing organizations from the antitrust laws. But the bloc's major effort was not in the area of regulation, but in assistance to marketing.

The basic problem was that many American farmers were overproducing, and yet could not compete on the world market. Some farmers talked of the possibility of a "two-price" system, with a high domestic price and a lower price for exports, with the government paying the farmers the difference between the two prices in one way or another. George N. Peek of the Moline (Illinois) Plow Company developed a somewhat similar idea, that included the concept of "parity" for agriculture with other sectors of the economy, while Hugh S. Johnson, also of Moline Plow, vigorously recommended it to farm organizations. Senator Charles McNary of Oregon and Representative Gilbert N. Haugen of Iowa added ideas of their own, and from this brew came the McNary-Haugen bill, first presented to Congress in 1924. The measure was supported by Coolidge's secretary of agriculture, Henry C. Wallace, but the president opposed it and the measure was defeated. Different versions of the bill were presented to Congress in 1927 and 1928, and they passed on both occasions, only to be vetoed by Coolidge as an unwarranted intrusion of government into the economy.

Hoover supported Coolidge in the vetoes. Indeed, more than anyone else in the cabinet he worked to defeat the various political solutions of the farm problem. So embroiled did Hoover become in the farm issue that upon Wallace's death in 1924 there was talk he would move from Commerce to Agriculture.[5] In fact Hoover, more than anyone else in the cabinet, framed agricultural policies in the 1920s.

Hoover saw no reason why the farmers could not solve their own problems without federal interference (*Alternative 6:* see Document 6). The key was cooperation and the associational movement. This not only would help protect the small farmers from being engulfed by larger units, but also lead to efficiency in operations and marketing, lowering prices to consumers, result in higher profits for farmers, and provide the United States with a more competitive position in world markets, all at the same time. In 1920 he said farmers needed "a better marketing system . . . better transportation system . . . development of a farm loan system . . . sane development of co-operative buying and selling among farmers . . . a development of our credit system to one that distinguishes between credits for speculative purposes and those for production and marketing of essentials in favor of the latter." The following year he worked with moderate farm bloc senators to help pass the Emergency Agricultural Credits Act, which among other things made possible federal loans to farm cooperatives and to foreign purchasers of American farm products, and he continued to speak in favor of such legislation throughout the 1920s. During the 1928 campaign Hoover said:

> My fundamental concept of agriculture is one controlled by its own members, organized to fight its own economic battles and to determine its own destinies. Nor do I speak of organization in the narrow sense of traditional farm co-operatives or pools, but in the much wider sense of a sound marketing organization. It is not by these proposals intended to put the Government into the control of the business of agriculture, nor to subsidize the prices of farm products and pay the losses thereon either by the Federal Treasury or by a tax or fee on the farmer. We propose with government assistance and an initial advance of capital to enable the agricultural industry to reach a stature of modern business operations by which the farmer will attain his independence and maintain his individuality.[6]

The vehicle for the plan already existed. Farm cooperatives proliferated in the 1920s. In 1915 there were fewer than six thousand of them; by 1926 there were more than twelve thousand, and the volume of business handled by the cooperatives increased more than one thousand percent to exceed $2.8 billion.

The cooperatives consisted of farmers with small and medium sized operations—and a few large ones at times—who united to market, buy, or pressure in unison. The Dairymen's League Co-operative Association furnished milk to a majority of New Yorkers; the Wisconsin Cheese Producers' Federation, with 299 members in 1929, had a national marketing structure. Land O'Lakes Creameries was the nation's largest butter marketer, while California cooperatives in fruit, prunes, apricots, and raisins dominated their fields. Sunkist, the orange cooperative, was a household name in 1929, when few urban Americans realized that cooperatives were coming to dominate several key agricultural areas.

As Hoover saw it, the cooperatives were to farming what the trade associations were to industry—groupings of like-minded individuals working together for the common good, promoting harmony and efficiency. Just as he endorsed federal approval of the associations, so he would have the government work through the cooperatives to help alleviate rural distress.

Hoover proposed the establishment of a nine-member Federal Farm Board which would be provided with a revolving fund of $500 million to grant loans to cooperatives and "stabilizing corporations" that would assist farmers in their purchasing, selling, financing, storing, and processing problems. The farm bloc legislators attempted to add a rider to the bill authorizing an export bounty, but Hoover, allied with the old guard, was able to beat it down. Most of them claimed the legislation, which was known as the Agricultural Marketing Act, was inadequate, although some saw in it a program that could be expanded at a later date. Yet so great was Hoover's reputation at the time that few would oppose him openly. Even Senator Norris went along with the idea, as probably the best that could be expected under the circumstances. The measure was approved in June, and Hoover signed it into law on June 15.[7]

A Vital Presidency

Hoover's actions during the campaign for the Agricultural Marketing Act were viewed as setting a pattern for executive-legislative relations during the rest of his administration. Hoover meant to lead Congress, as had Wilson and Roosevelt. But unlike them, he would do so by overwhelming his opponents by marshalling the facts of the case, by having superior knowledge of the issues involved, by being more logical. Hoover indicated his dislike for political maneuverings, although this too would be used when necessary and possible. Whenever he could, Hoover would approach a problem in a "scientific" fashion, transforming it into projects the engineering-business mind could comprehend and deal with, and then proceed to carry it through.[8] Now this had been done in the field of agriculture. The Marketing Act was only the first step in a complex program which, when completed, would restore prosperity to the farms while at the same time keeping the government's role to a minimum. At least, this seemed to be Hoover's hope in 1929.

The president's conservation program was the second aspect of the solution. While working on the Marketing Act, his staff completed work on several major dam and reclamation projects, but only those which private enterprise was unwilling to undertake and Hoover felt were needed. The president was also interested in expanding the nation's canal system and improving water transportation in general, in a way that would provide farmers with "a new instrument of commerce," and so ease their marketing problems. Federal construction programs, considered political plums in previous administrations, now expanded rapidly, and would continue to do so in every year of the Hoover administration. For the most part, however, the economy and Hoover's conception of government-business relations, and not politics, dictated contract awards.

During those first months in office scarcely a week would pass without the announcement of the selection of a new commission to study a problem, present a report, and recommend legislation. Expertness, facts, coordination—the hallmarks of business—became the style of the administration. Given such leadership, Hoover felt, any problem could be solved. He would spend federal funds to accomplish this, with a free hand if necessary, but as always, to help people help themselves.

Hoover was also aware of the impact such spending would have on the economy. Urgent programs, such as farmer-related construction, would be approved as soon as possible. But nonessential construction might be deferred, to be used to help boost the economy during recessions. In 1921 he had " . . . suggested that the first strategic point of attack was that Government construction should be so regulated that it may be deferred in times of intense private construction and expedited in times of unemployment." This too made good business sense; building in bad years would "secure more economical construction for the Government," while at the same time "mitigate unemployment in periods of depression."[9]

This was a new attitude in the federal executive branch. The combination of science, personal popularity, and activism made Hoover appear a strong man in the late summer of 1929. By then some Democratic newspapers were charging that Hoover had dictatorial ambitions, meant to crush the legislature, and was on his way to domination over all aspects of government. Hoover's supporters claimed that America had changed drastically during the past decade, creating a need for a new approach to meet new problems, or to transform the old ones in such a way that they finally could be resolved. Hoover was doing just that, they claimed, and needed new powers to accomplish his goals.[10]

The Tariff Debates

The conflict came to a head in the tariff debates during the April special session of Congress. Throughout the nineteenth and into the twentieth century the tariff had been considered one of the most vital matters with which Congress dealt. In 1929 Hoover asked for tariff revision in order to help the farmers, as part of his program to alleviate agrarian distress. But at the same time he hoped to gain power over rate setting. The tariff commission, under executive control, had been created in 1916. Under the terms of the Fordney-McCumber Tariff of 1922 the commission had been given minor powers to alter rates under special circumstances. Now Hoover wanted even greater flexibility and power "to revise the tariff to the differences in cost of production at home and abroad." In the future the commission, and not Congress, would have the major role in determining rates, which would be set "scientifically," without reference to politics.

Hoover believed in a protective tariff, as did most Republicans of his day, and as the party itself had since its inception. The tariff would protect American workers against the "slave labor" of the rest of the world, defend the high standard of living, and safeguard employment. Although reformers had long considered the tariff one of the most flagrant intrusions of government into the economy, Hoover either rejected or refused to consider that view. Instead, he wanted a tariff that would change to meet new conditions. On September 24 he said, " . . . if a perfect tariff bill were enacted the rapidity of our changing economic conditions and the constant shifting of our relations with economic life abroad would render some items in such an act imperfect in some particular within a year."[11]

The argument appeared reasonable, and won acceptance among many in big business, as well as farmers. In the past businessmen had relied upon compliant congressmen to pass tariff schedules to their liking. Now the schedules could be revised much more rapidly, with less trouble and politicking, by a commission selected by a business-minded president. Of course, there were dangers too. Who would succeed Hoover in 1937, after his second term? Might not a Democrat use the commission to lower rates? But this did not appear a real threat in the summer of 1929, when magazines were running articles asking whether the Democratic party could survive into 1932.

There were three major sources of opposition to the Hoover proposals, which were embodied in an inflexible high tariff bill introduced by Representative Willis C. Hawley of Oregon in June. Nonbusiness economists applauded the idea of flexibility, but at the same time noted that the United States was exporting far more than it was importing and that prices of manufactured goods had not fallen as much as they might have. In order to rectify an unsound trade imbalance and alleviate the price situation, tariffs should be lowered. Some farm bloc representatives, still supporting the McNary-Haugen measures, attempted to tack them on to the Hawley bill. Finally, legislators as a group were uneasy with the idea of shifting tariff powers from Capitol Hill to the White House. To them, this was another sign of Hoover's power grabbing activities. As a result, Hoover did not get his new tariff bill from the special session.

Preparation for Recession

The economy appeared strong when Hoover took office in March, 1929, but there were fears a new recession was in the wings. Economic growth in the 1920s had not been unalloyed; there had been minor dips in 1924 and 1927. After each dip, business had recovered rapidly, and then gone on to set new records. After the last such recession, Hoover had urged Coolidge to commission a group of experts to study the economy. The president agreed, and in January, 1928, the Committee on Recent Economic Changes met for the first time. Hoover was chairman of the group which consisted of leading businessmen and economists. Its work was completed in February, 1929, and the final report released soon after.

The report was generally optimistic, but the optimism was guarded. The past decade had seen major changes in the economy, due not primarily to new inventions, but to an acceleration of the pace of life and changes in distribution and consumption habits. Business strength was of major importance:

> The "self-policing" of business, with its codes of ethics, has been assisted by the recent development of trade-associations and the increasing influence of research and professional education. The strength and stability of our financial structure, both governmental and commercial, is of modern growth. The great corporate development of business enterprise, well marked in the fourth period of expansion, has gone on to new heights. It may be creating, a new type of social organization, but in any case, the open-mindedness of the public, and of the state which is its instrument, toward this growing power of business corporations appears to be novel in American history.

America was evolving, then, into something new, the shape of which could not be clearly discerned, but which was centered on the corporation. The business civilization was coming into its own, under the business president. Still, there were difficulties ahead.

> Here are the beginnings of new answers to the old problems. But more than this. Some of the basic elements of the problem are evidently in the process of change. The resources of the country, still enormous, are no longer regarded as limitless; the labor of the world is no longer invited freely to exploit them. The capital flow has turned outward; private and public interests and responsibilities have a new world-wide scope. These changes must have far-reaching consequences and entail further and more perplexing adjustments.[12]

The committee did not suggest what these adjustments should or would be, but it was clear from this and other selections that many of the group thought a major growth era was ending. The nation was entering a new period during which it would be a world power, both politically and economically. Whether or not growth would continue in this new period was questioned, but not answered.

At the same time, others seeking a narrower and less philosophical focus, believed the workings of the business cycle might lead to a dip in the near future. Economist Wesley C. Mitchell, the nation's leading expert on the cycle, warned of this in his review of the situation in early 1929. The cycle could be dampened, especially through vigorous political and economic countermeasures, but it could not be eliminated. As he saw it, the nation could be in for another 1921.

> That we have not had a serious crisis since 1920 or a severe depression since 1921 is no guarantee that we shall be equally prudent, skillful and

fortunate in the years to come. If we are to maintain business prosperity, we must continue to earn it month after month and year after year by intelligent effort. The incomes disbursed to consumers, and to wage earners in particular, must be increased on a scale sufficient to pay for the swelling volume of consumers' goods sent to market. The credit structure must be kept in due adjustment to the earnings of business enterprises. Security prices must not outrun prospective profits capitalized as the going rate of interest. Commodity stocks must be held in line with current sales. Over-commitments of all sorts must be avoided. The building of new industrial equipment must not be overrapid. These and similar matters which might be mentioned present delicate problems of management which will find their practical solutions in the daily decisions of business executives. Perhaps errors are being kept within the limits of tolerance. Perhaps no serious setback will occur for years to come. But we are leaving 1921 well behind us, and there are signs that the caution inspired by that disastrous year is wearing thin.[13]

A replay of 1920-1921 appeared quite possible in early 1929. Mitchell ably catalogued the reasons—stock market speculation; workers whose wages did not enable them to purchase the goods they produced, thus creating gluts in supply; a shaky credit structure; and overbuilding. All had been present in 1919. Now, it appeared, "history was repeating itself."

But it need not be as bad as 1921, this depression that might be coming. The nation had learned much since then, and appeared far stronger. Business had developed sophisticated techniques to counter adverse trends, and together with government, could dampen the effects of such a depression. Finally, there was the man in the White House. Hoover was no Wilson, debating the League of Nations while his own nation was falling apart, or a Harding, well-meaning and amiable, but without a clear understanding of economic forces. Instead, he was of a new breed, the technician-businessman, capable of solving all problems. Hoover had demonstrated his strength during the special session; his devotion to liberty was well-known, as was his work as a humanitarian. Depressions were technical problems. If and when another 1920-1921 situation developed, who was better equipped than Hoover to solve it?

Notes

1. On coming to office Hoover promised to hold regular press conferences that would be more open than any in the past. At first they were, but when sharp questions were asked, Hoover refused to respond. Within a few months the conferences deteriorated and were scheduled with diminishing frequency. This added to Hoover's "credibility gap." See Robert S. Allen and Drew Pearson, *Washington Merry-Go-Round* (New York: H. Liveright, Inc., 1931) for a view of the capital in the early Hoover administration.

2. In this regard, Hoover resembled Wilson who, however, had a better and more varied political background. Wilson believed himself the intellectual superior of his congressional opponents as well as being morally elevated, while Hoover assumed his knowledge and approach was more "scientific" than those of his congressional opponents. Neither man believed strongly in the division of federal powers, rhetoric to the contrary notwithstanding. But Wilson had been able, at least initially, to *lead* Congress. Hoover was not.

3. On occasion, the term "Sons of the Wild Jackass" was used to signify membership in the farm bloc, since they were constantly "braying" about the problem. By 1928,

however, it alluded more often to the former progressives, some of whom considered farm problems of secondary importance.

4. Michelson was quite frank about his role. See Charles Michelson, *The Ghost Talks* (New York: G.P. Putnam's Sons, 1944).

5. In his memoirs, Hoover described Wallace as a "dour Scotsman with a temperament inherited from some ancestor who had been touched by exposure to infant damnation and predestination. He made much trouble for the Department of Commerce." He saw in Wallace the tentacles of an alien ideology. "Facism has blossomed in Italy. Its buds were swelling in the United States, with demands from the left wing that government should fix prices, wages, production, and distribution. This was no less an invasion of liberty than Socialism. We had to meet it constantly in direct or indirect attempts at legislation. My colleague, the Secretary of Agriculture, was in truth a facist, he did not know it, when he proposed his price- and distribution-fixing legislation in the McNary-Hagen bill." Herbert C. Hoover, *The Memoirs of Herbert Hoover: The Cabinet and the Presidency, 1920-1933* (New York: Macmillan, 1951), pp. 109, 174.

6. Ray L. Wilbur and Arthur M. Hyde, *The Hoover Policies* (New York: C. Scribner's Sons, 1937), pp. 147-50.

7. Alexander Legge of International Harvester, who had worked harmoniously with Hoover during the war, was named chairman of the Federal Farm Board. At the time he said, "What the Board hopes to do is to assist farmers to become better able to compete with other groups in the markets of the nation and the world. It expects by aiding in the development of cooperative associations to make possible economies in marketing and stabilized marketing conditions, and to assist farmers to obtain their just share of the national income." This statement, together with an excellent analysis of the politics of agriculture in 1929, may be found in Albert U. Romansco, *The Poverty of Abundance: Hoover, the Nation, the Depression* (New York: Oxford University Press, 1965), chapter 6.

8. In 1920 Hoover said: "I sometimes feel that public problems can be divided into two classes. The first is that in which sufficient facts, figures, or concrete experience can be amassed to give certain indication of the course of constructive action. The second are those arising out of sheer complexes of political, economic and social currents, in which solution at best is more largely pure judgment guided by adherence to national ideals. The common judgment must arise out of common discussion, the development of a common mind flowing from the common sense of the people. The latter type of problem seems to especially lend itself to destructive criticism. The greatness of this country, however, has not grown from the police court mind." Wilbur and Hyde, *The Hoover Policies*, p. 41.

9. Hoover, *Memoirs: Cabinet and Presidency*, p. 175.

10. Press comment on the Agricultural Marketing Act and the tariff debates may best be followed in the *Literary Digest* for 1919.

11. Wilbur and Hyde, *The Hoover Policies*, p. 183.

12. Committee on Recent Economic Changes, *Recent Economic Changes in the United States* (New York: McGraw-Hill, 1929), pp. 11-12.

13. Ibid., p. 910.

4

Challenge and Response

There is a popular myth that the nation was struck unaware by the stock market crash of October, 1929 and the coming of the Great Depression, which ended the New Era and ushered in the New Deal. One is given a picture of a nation engaged in the vanities and excesses of the Jazz Age, suddenly plunged into the worst economic and social calamity Americans had ever known. It is almost biblical in tone—the sins of the seven good years atoned for by the sorrows of the seven bad ones. And a Calvinist, Social Darwinist people, which prefers its symbols painted in primary colors without shadings in between, has accepted this myth. Even those who warned of the depression are assigned a biblical role, as prophets crying in the wilderness, with none to listen until it was too late.

The facts of the situation were quite different. Ever since the postwar depression, American scholars and some politicians had been concerned with the business cycle, and attempted to counteract it in such a way as to alleviate its excesses. In 1921-1922 the Harding administration let out government contracts for construction, in the hope of boosting employment and pumping purchasing power into the economy. For the first time the federal government used its muscle in a time of economic distress, although it was employed sparingly. Senator William S. Kenyon introduced legislation calling upon the president to consider the use of public works projects in future depressions. The measure was defeated, despite strong backing by Hoover, who was in charge of the Harding antidepression efforts in 1921-1922. Many congressmen considered it "socialistic."

In 1928 Senator Wesley Jones of Washington, believing America was headed into another depression, introduced a stronger version of the Kenyon proposals, which was also defeated. Senator Robert Wagner of New York proposed an even more sweeping set of measures, which included the establishment of federally-sponsored employment agencies in time of distress, the compilation of better economic statistics than were then available, and the advanced planning of public works, to be put into effect when the president felt them necessary as a counter-cyclical measure. Candidate and later President-elect Hoover supported the last two proposals, but rejected the idea of federal employment agencies. This was consistent with his view that the government should not interfere in the private sector, but could act where private enterprise was unable to. It also indicated that Hoover, more than any previous occupant of the White House, was willing to utilize federal power in times of depression.

In November, 1928, the regularly-scheduled Governors' Conference convened in New Orleans. Hoover had just scored his triumph at the polls, and talk of his plans dominated the discussions. Governor Ralph Brewster of Maine, telling the assembled governors that he was speaking for the president-elect, discussed the possibility of a new depression similar to that which had occurred in 1920-1921. "America is in a position to stabilize prosperity to a most remarkable extent," he said. "With the facts in hand, the expenditure of comparatively few millions in useful work may easily head off a depression that would cost a billion." Brewster suggested the governors back a plan to establish a reserve fund of $3 billion, to be used by the president for public works when early signs of depression were confirmed. The motion was rejected. Many governors felt it gave undue power to the president, while others believed the idea socialistic. The Brewster proposal confirmed the fears of many that Hoover meant to be a very strong president, stronger perhaps than any of his predecessors since Lincoln. He would gain this strength at their expense, and so they opposed him.

In early 1929 the Federal Reserve Board began issuing warnings against speculation, telling member banks they should not lend money for "speculative purposes." Newspapers carried stories of a slowdown in construction activity that spring, while retail sales also declined. Industrial production declined somewhat in July, and continued to fall in August and September, while unemployment rose in all three months. Clearly a business slowdown was at hand. The story was there to see, for all who read the business pages of major newspapers and government publications and statistics. In September the *Federal Reserve Bulletin* noted that "a considerable increase has taken place since the beginning of 1929 in the number of business concerns in difficulties."[1]

The Stock Market Crash

Meanwhile, securities prices continued to rise at the nation's stock exchanges. The Dow-Jones Industrials fell almost 29 points in March, only to advance by more than 82 points in the next three months. The Dow closed at 381.17 on September 3. This was to be the top of the bull market, almost two months prior to "Black Thursday." Now the averages headed downward. There was a sharp decline in mid-October, one many commentators called a "correction." From that point on the decline was steady, culminating with the disastrous Thursday trading.[2] It was a true financial panic. But at the time it was not perceived as a disaster.

Leading economists seemed to share this view. From Great Britain Josiah Stamp told reporters that the market crash would liquidate unsound investments, freeing funds for more productive uses. John Maynard Keynes believed that the credit push on Wall Street would be ended by the crash. Industry would now have more plentiful funds, which would be used for productive purposes, not speculation. Neither saw a major depression in the works. Financial writers at the New York *Times* thought it a good opportunity to buy "sound" stocks. The *Wall Street Journal* considered the crash a "shakeout," after which prices would firm and then rise once more. In an editorial on October 29 it set the tone for discussions during the next few weeks, and reflected the view Wall Street as a community held regarding the market and economy:

> It was a panic, a purely stock-market panic, of a new brand. Everyone seems to agree that it was due to the fact that prices of some stocks were selling beyond respective intrinsic values and a correction has taken place in a number of stocks that show declines ranging from 50 to more than 100 points. . . . The recent break was due to the position of the market itself. It came when money was 5 percent, with a plethora of funds available for lending purposes, normal inventories, corporations flush with surplus money, sound economic conditions, and so on. It is because of the fact that the slump was due to the market itself that the storm has left no wreckage except marginal traders forced to sell at a loss. Mr. [George F.] Baker, Mr. Morgan, Mr. Mellon, Mr. Rockefeller, and others who held stocks outright, stand just where they were before the break. Their income is the same. They have lost a few tail feathers but in time they will grow again, longer and more luxurious than the old ones that were lost in what financial writers like to call the debacle.

The *Guaranty Survey*, put out by the Guaranty Trust Company, believed that "viewed in the longer perspective, the collapse of the inflated price structure may be correctly regarded as a favorable development from the point of view of general business." "I can observe little on the horizon today to give us undue or great concern," said John E. Edgerton, president of the National Association of Manufacturers. In late December President James Farrell of U.S. Steel said, "It is confidently expected that after the turn of the year operations in the steel industry will substantially improve." Frederick Ecker of Metropolitan Life agreed. "Any slackness that may be apparent in the general business situation during the early months of 1930 can be attributed almost entirely to the hesitant state of mind in which business has been since the collapse of the stock market, rather than to any important change in the fundamental conditions."[3]

These men were not dissembling, or merely whistling in the dark. In fact, the economic and financial underpinning of the American economy did give the appearance of strength. Unemployment figures were not rising toward the end of 1929; fourth quarter business profits were good; breadlines did not appear on the streets. Stock prices did fall almost 70 points on the Dow Industrials in October, and another 34.5 in November. Then the market rallied, and by Christmas it was strong, rising almost 10 points in December. From December 1, 1929 to April 30, 1930, the Dow advanced more than 47 points. It was hardly a vigorous rally, but to those living through that period, it did not seem as though the market was finished, or the bull era dead.[4]

Most importantly, the banks held. During the great stock market panics of the past—the kinds that had ushered in major depressions, such as those of 1873, 1884, and especially 1893—bank failures proliferated. Not a single major bank closed its doors during the immediate aftermath of Black Thursday, nor did any seem in danger of closing. In 1929, 659 commercial banks suspended operations, fewer than in 1924, 1926, or 1927. So it did not seem another 1893, or even a 1907. Rather, to those involved in the day-to-day operations of Wall Street, and to most economists, it appeared a repetition of 1921.[5]

Alternative Responses

Believing this to be the case, many businessmen held that the government should take a hands-off policy toward the economy. Reflecting the old Social Darwinist beliefs, they thought the depression—sharp, short, and cutting— would force speculators, marginal operators, the weak and unfit, from the market place. The strong, wise, and prudent would survive. This was not only natural; it was correct. Any government interference would be not only ill-considered, but injurious. In 1920, National Association of Manufacturers President Edgerton averred that "neither society nor any human power can immunize anybody against the natural consequences of the violation of law—civil, moral, spiritual, or economic. Society cannot protect against the consequences of rejected or misused opportunity or thriftlessness." The unemployed, he went on to say, were individuals who had failed to perform well in society when jobs were there for the asking.

> There have been many more days when a well-paying job was available to everyone who wanted it than of those when any appreciable number could not find work. Many of those who are most boisterous now in clamor for work have either struck on the jobs they had or don't want to work at all, and are utilizing the occasion to swell the communistic chorus. If, then, during the larger number of more prosperous days, when everybody has the opportunity to work and earn more than enough for their actual needs, they do not foresee the demonstrated certainty of lean days ahead and practice their habits of thrift and conservation, or if they gamble away their savings in the stock markets or elsewhere, is our economic system, or government, or industry to blame? What system or government can keep people from being fools or going crazy?[6]

Edgerton was echoed by many business leaders in the early days of the depression. To them it seemed such business declines, by purging the unfit from their ranks, would have a salubrious effect. The most striking statement of this belief came from Secretary of the Treasury Mellon. He told Hoover of his recollections of the great depression of the 1870s, which he thought far worse than anything that was happening in late 1929. Mass unemployment was the rule; tens of thousands of farms had been foreclosed; few banks were open. In time, however, business inventories were worked off, and orders came to the plants, whose owners—the wise and prudent ones who survived the hard times—then employed men and set the wheels of industry turning again. Mellon urged Hoover to maintain a hands-off policy.

> Let the slump liquidate itself. Liquidate labor, liquidate stocks, liquidate the farmers, liquidate real estate.... It will purge the rottenness out of the system. High costs of living and high living will come down. People will work harder, live a more moral life. Values will be adjusted, and enterprising people will pick up from less competent people.[7]

A minority of businessmen thought the depression would not be ended by one of Mellon's healthful "purges." Rather, it was a sign that the nation had reached a major turning point, that laissez faire free enterprise was outmoded and had to be replaced by a new philosophy stressing planning and business-government cooperation. The antitrust laws would have to be repealed, and the wastes brought about by competition eliminated. Gerard Swope, president of General Electric, began speaking in early 1930 of what he would later label "the stabilization of industry," in which wages would be set by government, employment guaranteed to workers, and businessmen organized in large units to run their own industries. "We have left the period of extreme individualism," said Henry I. Harriman of the New England Power Company. Later he would say, "Business prosperity and employment will be best maintained by an intelligently planned business structure."

A significant number of intellectuals analyzed the situation along lines similar to Harriman and Swope's reasoning, but came to different con-clusions. The Socialists called for the formation of a new party that would replace the Democrats (in much the same way as Labour replaced the Liberals in Britain), and then go on to sweep the Republicans out of office in 1932, and institute a socialist state. "Take Communism from the Communists," said Edmund Wilson. The Soviet Union had defects, he thought, but it remained "the moral top of the world where the light never really goes out." Wilson and others like him saw the nation at a great divide, with fascism on the one side and communism on the other. Liberals, reformers, conservatives, and their kin fell between, offering no real alternative.

For the moment, at least, Wilson seemed perceptive. Congressional reformers, such as Bob LaFollette, Fiorello LaGuardia, George Norris, and William Borah spoke as though the tariff and public power were at the top of the agenda of reform. Not until 1931 would such men sponsor general relief legislation, and then only in a halfhearted fashion. Senator Thomas Gore, a liberal and reformer, thought even then that reform would prove a weak reed. The depression would not be ended by laws or resolutions, he said; it could not be cured in this way any more "than you can pass a resolution to prevent disease. This is an economic disease. You might just as well try to prevent the human race from having a disease as to prevent economic grief of this sort."[8]

What was the alternative? Gore did not say. Some businessmen were proposing a benign form of fascism, and expressed admiration of Mussolini, while reformers were opting for Soviet-style solutions or, for the most part, saying little.

The Hoover Response

Hoover appeared to have no doubts as to the meaning of the crash and the depression that followed. Shortly after Black Thursday, he told the nation that "the fundamental business of the country—that is, the production and distribution of goods and services—is on a sound and prosperous basis." Later on it would be claimed that Hoover said this in order to calm fears and stem panic. His actions in the months that followed, however, indicate that he truly believed this to have been the case. The economy was in fine shape, even though there were minor weaknesses here and there, problems he had tried to meet during the special session of Congress held the previous spring. Should these problems persist, he had developed the tools necessary to correct them. Meanwhile there were two sick areas that had to be isolated from the rest of the economy. He would take actions to do this, while at the same time putting into operation counter-cyclical programs as a sort of antibiotic for the body politic (*Alternative 6:* see Document 6).

Hoover had been a man who, throughout his prepresidential career, had distrusted non-Americans and praised hard work. Perhaps it was natural, then, that he would identify foreigners and stock market speculators as the two principle sources of the depression.

Throughout the 1920s Hoover had warned against speculation in securities. In 1926 he spoke often of "the fever of speculation." "Disturbances from this quarter may at once interfere with the fundamental business of producing goods and distributing them," he warned.

As president, Hoover did what he could to curb speculation. At his request Secretary Mellon issued warnings against the Wall Street fever, and Henry Robinson, president of the First Security National Bank of Los Angeles, was dispatched to the financial district as a presidential emissary to the investment banking community, to ask for its cooperation in halting the boom. Hoover called Stock Exchange president Richard Whitney to the White House and asked him to do what he could in the same direction, and he spoke with prominent editors and publishers, asking them to print articles and editorials on the subject. Hoover did not go beyond his powers as president to interfere with Wall Street activities, and he did not ask Congress for new powers in that field. To do so might precipitate a crash, even had Hoover thought new powers necessary. But the record of the first seven months of the Hoover administration vis-à-vis the stock market is clear: Hoover did more to pressure the financial district into compliance with presidential wishes than had any of his predecessors.

The second sick area was Europe—in 1952 Hoover would call it "the great storm center." Britain had been in economic difficulties since 1925. Germany and France had entered a downward economic cycle in 1928-1929, as had other countries. In Hoover's view, this was caused in large part by "enormous war destruction, the economic consequences of the Peace of Versailles, revolutions, unbalanced budgets, hugely increased armaments, inflation, the gigantic overproduction of rubber, coffee, and other commodities, through overstimulation from artificial controls, and a score of other aftermaths of the war. . . .[9] By mid-1929 the European disease had contaminated the United States." Now a quarantine was needed.

The quarantine came in the form of tariff revision. Discussion of the revision had begun during the special session, and was continued when Congress reconvened in December, 1929, at a time when the stock market was recovering, Christmas sales in department stores attracted good business, and the depression itself under control.

The initial debates had taken place at a time when the country seemed headed for permanent prosperity; they were revived when economic stability appeared shaken. Originally, Hoover, like Harding before him, had viewed the tariff as a means of assisting farmers, an integral part of a complex program that included creation of the Federal Farm Board. In addition, he had insisted on flexibility in rate setting, which would enable the Tariff Commission, presumably under his control, to set rates within a wide range. His reformist opponents had insisted on attaching subsidy and marketing riders to the bill, reflecting the McNary-Haugen mentality, and so the measure—the original Hawley Tariff bill—had gone down to defeat.

By December, however, the tariff appeared to be a measure that could isolate America from Europe economically. High tariff advocates, rather subdued the previous summer, now came to the fore. They were led by Senator Joseph Grundy of Pennsylvania, a newly-seated but powerful legislator, who was also president of the Pennsylvania Manufacturers' Association and a force in the Republican party. Under Grundy's direction, many rates were raised, and a mildly protectionist schedule was transformed into one of the highest in American history. Hawley said it would make the nation "self-contained and self-sustaining." His Senate cosponsor, Reed Smoot, thought that under it, the nation would achieve "a high degree of self-sufficiency," and so need not trouble with foreigners.

Hoover said little regarding the rate changes, but concentrated instead on the flexibility issue. He sparred with Grundy and the old guard for months on this issue and in the end prevailed. Hoover received his strong Tariff Commission. But at the same time, the rates remained high.

The president was severely criticized for accepting the bill; a petition signed by one thousand professional economists was published, urging him to veto it. This and other protests prompted him to respond in some detail. On June 15, 1930, he said he would approve the measure as fulfillment of campaign promises made in 1928. He defended the Hawley-Smoot Tariff, claiming its schedule was actually somewhat lower than previous ones, and saying that the flexibility provision, not the schedule, was its most significant feature. Hoover also implied that he would maintain high rates, high enough to protect American businessmen and workers against foreign competition.

> If a perfect tariff bill were enacted today, the increasing rapidity of economic change and the constant shifting of our relations to industries abroad will create a continuous stream of items which would work hardship upon some segment of the American people except for the provision of this relief. Without a workable flexible provision we would require even more frequent Congressional tariff revision than during the past. With it the country should be freed from further general revision for many years to come. Congressional revisions are not only disturbing to business but, with all their necessary collateral surroundings in lobbies, logrolling, and the activities of group interests, are disturbing to public confidence. . . .[10]

Together with continued speeches on the general soundness of the economy—speeches designed to restore confidence on Wall Street, among other things—the Hawley-Smoot Tariff "isolated the patient" for treatment. Even while he was acting on these two fronts, the president placed his program into operation.

Hoover had a presidential program to offer the nation, one without congressional assistance or support. At no time in the next year—the period from October, 1929 to April, 1931—did he ask Congress for important new legislation, or attempt to share responsibility for his actions. This was not unusual; Roosevelt in 1907, and Cleveland in 1893, had behaved similarly. In 1921 Harding had followed the same pattern. Still, all three had been subjected to congressional criticism after the fact; had Congress been given obligations and responsibilities, Hoover might have escaped the onslaught that came in 1931-1932.

On the other hand, there was no indication that congressional leaders had any desire to offer their own plans to halt the slump. The reformers were quiet; not until early 1930 would they offer programs, and then usually rehashes of old ones, such as Wagner's tripartite plan for employment agencies and federal works. Democratic leaders spoke of the need for a balanced budget; this was Representative John Nance Garner's pet peeve. Senator Joseph Robinson of Arkansas, a leader in the upper house, thought the nation should "sit steady in the boat." He told Democrat Bernard Baruch that "I grow more and more impressed with the necessity of conservative action . . . " and Baruch responded that "No government agency . . . can cure this situation." On the other hand, Baruch believed the depression would be short-lived; Hoover would be "fortunate enough, before the next election, to have a rising tide and then he will be pictured as the great master mind who led the country out of its economic misery."

Old guard Republicans showed no desire to offer alternatives to Hoover programs. Senator David Reed of Pennsylvania warned against "legislative quackery" and "fussy governmental muddling." "By the workings of natural forces and the collective good sense of the American people . . . we shall recover our economic equilibrium." Senator Hiram Bingham of Connecticut rephrased Grover Cleveland's dictum, saying: "It is not the business of Washington to look out for the general welfare of the States. It is the business of the States to look out for the general welfare of the people." Senator Simeon Fess of Ohio believed no legislation was needed since the depression would not last long. In 1930 he declared "it has been a rather good thing for the country and in thirty days from now probably we will not know there was such a thing." Meanwhile, the nation had to "sit steady and make the best of a bad situation." Like the reformers, the old guard could only offer rewarmed programs and old panaceas in 1929-1930. Reed Smoot wanted to raise the tariff even higher; Bingham said that "repeal [of prohibition] is the one thing which will restore prosperity." Reed wanted an end to immigration, so that native-born Americans would not lose jobs to aliens.[11]

Within a year all three congressional factions—reformers, old guard Republicans, and moderate Democrats—would criticize Hoover harshly for his actions and the lack of them. At no time in that first year, however, did any of them offer an alternative, or indicate that they, like the president, believed the depression would last more than a few months, or a year at worst.

The Hoover Program

Hoover believed his program would help the nation over the "rough spots"—a term used by many commentators to describe the depression in late 1929. The program was grounded upon cooperation between businessmen and labor leaders, and assistance by governments. It was a direct outgrowth of the associational activities Hoover had been involved in throughout the 1920s, based on his belief in the innate desire for liberty held by Americans, and faith in the ability of enlightened self-interest and modern economics to deal with complex phenomena. The federal government would bring the elements of the economy together, outline the problems, provide expertness, and in this way end the depression (*Alternative 8:* see Documents 7 and 8).

This general policy was quite different from those previous presidents had followed when faced with economic downturns. Grover Cleveland and Theodore Roosevelt used the rhetoric of laissez faire and depended upon business leadership to end the financial panics; at most they would cooperate with business, and even accept its leadership. Hoover rejected this attitude. He was an activist in 1929-1930, even more so later on. And if this activism meant the use of counter-cyclical economics, he was prepared to follow it. He cut the income taxes (not a major item in 1929-1930, however) and went so far as to accept deficit financing. The federal budget showed a slight surplus in 1929 and 1930 and Hoover was proud of it. But he accepted large deficits in 1931 and 1932. In 1932 the deficit was $2.7 billion, the largest in peacetime history to that time.

Hoover believed purchasing power had to be preserved. Toward this end, he encouraged manufacturers to maintain wages and employment, and asked union leaders to cooperate in the efforts. This, more than anything else, would restore public confidence in the economy. The public had to understand that "something" was being done to end the downturn, while at the same time individual liberties were being preserved.

State and local officials were to cooperate with the private sector whenever their help was needed. In addition, they were to assist in private efforts and relief for the poor. Hoover believed self-help was the answer here. The community should unite to aid those in need, on a temporary basis. The president, who had headed the largest public relief effort in history during the Great War, would use federal powers if necessary. But in 1929, these were not deemed important to a depression situation that would pass shortly.

The federal government's *direct* role would be twofold. In the first place, the Federal Reserve, through open market operations and reduction of the discount rate, would increase the money supply and create an atmosphere of "easy money," thus preserving liquidity. This role had been taken by J.P. Morgan in the 1893 and 1907 panics. Morgan was dead, and Wall Street had thrown up no one of similar power and authority. When Woodrow Wilson talked of central banking in 1913, he indicated that in crisis times, it could and should act as Hoover was using it in 1929.

Hoover also expanded public construction, and urged private builders to do the same. Ever since 1921 he had indicated this was the "greatest tool which our economic system affords for the establishment of stability." Statements such as this reinforce the conclusion that Hoover, like almost everyone else in power as well as their critics, had failed to grasp the seriousness of the situation in late 1929. On the other hand, had the analysis been correct, and the depression ended in a year or so, Hoover might have been chastised for grabbing and using too much power in 1929-1930, for in that period he proved a more activist president than any since the wartime activities of Wilson and Lincoln. Indeed, no peacetime president since Jefferson had done more to expand the powers of the presidency than Hoover had in that one year.

The White House held a series of conferences beginning on November 19, when the president met with a group of railroad presidents. Then came industrialists, labor leaders, governors, mayors, and organizers of private relief efforts. The New York *Times* said they were "the largest gathering of noted heads of industrial and other corporations in Washington since the resources of the nation were marshalled for participation in the World War." Hoover called the meetings "the Conference for Continued Industrial Progress." Within a nine day period he held seven of these meetings, attended by such prominent figures as Henry Ford, Alfred Sloan, Jr., John L. Lewis, William Green, and Pierre du Pont. After each meeting an optimistic statement was released to the press. The president said, "It was considered that the development of cooperative spirit and responsibility in the American business world was such that the business of the country itself could and should assume the responsibility for the mobilization of the industrial and commercial agencies to these ends and to cooperate with the governmental agencies." Toward this end, he named Chairman Julius H. Barnes of the United States Chamber of Commerce to head a central executive committee made up of leading spokesmen for the business community.

On December 5 the committee's work was ready, and the National Business Survey Conference was held in Washington. Hoover addressed the members, telling them they were there "to create a temporary organization for the purpose of systematically spreading into industry as a whole the measures which have been taken by some of our leading industries to counteract the effect of the recent panic in the stock market."

The efforts were quite simple and direct: all the participants agreed to maintain employment and wages, not only to keep the economy working, but as a sign of their confidence in recovery. For the most part, the industrialists honored these pledges throughout 1930, and in the case of some—Henry

Ford, for example— actually instituted wage increases in the face of declining sales and profits. But in late 1930, when it appeared the depression might be long-lived, the agreements began to crumble.

While encouraging private efforts of this kind, Hoover initiated his long-planned public works projects. In January, 1930, he authorized work on Boulder Dam that would cost $60 million. Another $75 million went to highway programs, and $500 million for public buildings. "Our drive for increase in construction and improvement work to take up unemployment is showing most encouraging results," he told the press on January 3, "and it looks as if the work undertaken will be larger for 1930 than for 1929." (Later on he observed that during past depressions, the presidents had cut back on construction to balance the budget.) He increased spending substantially, and the increases continued in every year of his administration, rising from $410 million in 1930 to $656 million in 1932. In addition to this, Hoover encouraged the private sector to speed up their construction programs, and here too the cooperative approach worked. On December 2, 1930, Hoover reported that private construction that year would amount to around $7 billion, against $6.3 billion in 1929.

Hoover's construction efforts, something new in American political history, were applauded by businessmen and criticized by congressional Democrats and a portion of the press. The former viewed counter-cyclical construction as an intelligent method of ironing out the business cycle— business had used the method for decades within their own firms. [12] Opposition Democrats and reformers charged Hoover with using federal funds to reward friends with fat contracts; there was little note of the economic impact of the program, and Hoover proved inept at publicizing it.

By October, 1929, almost one-third of all farmers were members of one or more cooperative associations. These, according to Hoover, would be the major vehicles for recovery. The Farmers' National Grain Corporation, established with federal help in October, was equipped to assist grain farmers in almost every aspect of their business, and the president envisaged other, similar organizations, that would do the same for all farmers in time. In 1930, for example, the government helped establish the National Fruit and Vegetable Exchange and the National Beet Growers Association. At the same time, Alexander Legge at the Federal Farm Board attempted to assist cotton growers by urging them to withhold their crop from market until prices rose, offering low interest loans to hold them over until then. In February, 1930, Hoover established the Grain Stabilization Corporation to help the wheat farmers. Cooperation between labor and capital would maintain prices and employment; cooperation between farmers and marketers, together with federal loans, would do the same for the agricultural sector.

The Failure on the Farms

The farm problem, deeper and more complex than the difficulties in industry, defied this solution. So on March 6, Hoover proceeded with direct intervention, through federal wheat purchases carried out by the Grain Stabilization Corporation. This was an unprecedented move; never before had the federal government intervened so directly into the private sector. Legge explained to critics that the Stabilization Corporation was not a *federal* agency, but rather one controlled and directed by farmers. But the funding was federal, a fact Legge attempted to underplay. He said that the Farm Board "is prepared to advance to this farmers' organization, whatever funds are necessary . . ." By June, the Farm Board owned sixty-five million bushels of wheat, either directly or through the purchase of future contracts, at a cost of $90 million.

Hoover had gone beyond the hopes of the McNary-Haugen advocates of the 1920s in assisting farmers. As was the case in industry, he was roundly criticized for his actions. Old guard Republicans thought he was destroying private enterprise on the farms; reformers and opposition Democrats charged federal funds were being used to reward the president's political friends. Yet neither offered viable alternatives or even cogent criticisms of the plan or its philosophy.

The farm states were struck by a major drought in 1930, one that both helped and complicated the situation. Production of several crops declined, although wheat figures were higher than those of 1929. The cutback helped stabilize prices, although the decline continued, as it had throughout the 1920s. But in addition, the drought resulted in widespread hardship and even starvation in the plains states.

This presented Hoover with a human rather than economic problem. He would not intercede directly to help farmers in economic difficulty—this would cripple their self-reliance and individual liberties. But people in distress were another matter. Viewing the situation as comparable to those he had faced in World War I, he helped organize relief efforts. A Federal Drought Relief Committee, headed by Secretary of Agriculture Arthur Hyde, was quickly established to distribute loans to needy farmers, and in October the National Association of Commissioners of Agriculture met in Washington to help draft new relief legislation. Meanwhile, Hoover conferred with the presidents of railroads operating in the drought areas and obtained a fifty percent reduction in rates for foodstuffs being shipped to the destitute. The highway program in these areas was speeded up to provide employment for destitute farmers.

This was to be the limit of federal intervention (Documents 6 and 8). Hoover's belief in self-help, volunteerism, and the associational movement was transformed in this case into a strong support of the Red Cross, which in January, 1931, he called "the Nation's sole agency for relief in such a crisis." The Red Cross allocated $5 million to meet the crisis, and Hoover lent his support to a special drive to raise an additional $10 million. Red Cross Chairman John B. Payne told Hoover that his organization was "prepared to relieve actual distress in the premises," but in fact lacked the organization, manpower, and funds for the task in 1930, and was little better prepared in 1931.

The matter of aid to drought victims aroused congressional reformers who, allied with normally conservative legislators from the stricken states, united to support proposals for federal intervention. The fact that 1930 was an election year served to precipitate the discontent. Congressmen returning to their homes to campaign found an increasing number of their constituents less interested in liberty, freedom, and Social Darwinist sentiments than in food, clothing, and shelter. Raskob and Michelson made the depression the issue in 1930, even more so than it would have been. Michelson painted Hoover as an unfeeling man, an incompetent, who had to be retired from office if the depression was to be ended. Only a few months earlier, the president had been criticized for being too much of an activist; now he was castigated for his refusal to use power.

Democratic Representative Robert Doughton of North Carolina campaigned against Hoover and for direct relief in 1930. But he knew that had his own party been in office, conditions would not have been otherwise. "Were the Democrats in power . . . we could not get started on a race in this campaign." Arthur Capper of Kansas, a ranking GOP senator, thought his party was "going to get the damnedest licking it has had for a long time . . ."[13] Yet the defeat was not as bad as had been anticipated, and considering that the party in power usually loses off-year elections, the results were surprisingly good. In the new Senate there would be 48 Republicans, 47 Democrats, and one Farmer-Laborite, while in the House there would be 218 Republicans, 216 Democrats, and one Farmer-Laborite. The new Congress would not meet until December, 1931, however, and by then deaths would swing majorities to the Democrats.

Democratic leaders pledged support to the president after the election, but at the same time opened their barrage of criticism on the relief issue. Senator Joseph Robinson of Arkansas, who had been Smith's vice-presidential running mate in 1928, joined with the party's leader in the House, John N. Garner of Texas, in calling for direct aid, not loans, to farmers. Senator Borah, the leader of the Republican progressives, castigated the president for his lack of action on the issue, and other progressives joined in. Meanwhile, the old guard either lost confidence in Hoover or considered his actions too activistic, and did not defend him. The press, never pro-Hoover except on the surface, joined in. By early 1931, the president was isolated, with little support from the opposition, and not much more from his own party in Congress.

Hoover picked up the challenge on relief after the election, as though determined to stand or fall on it. If he had deliberately selected the poorest possible field for battle, he could not have done worse, for the election results and public comment appeared to indicate a swing of opinion against him on the matter. On the other hand, direct relief offered a clear area for a discussion of his philosophy of government and the individual, and Hoover accepted the challenge on that basis. Politically, it was an unwise decision. But Hoover was never known for his political acumen. Instead, he liked to think of himself as a defender of what he was now calling "the American Way" against foreign ideologies. Increasingly during this post election period he spoke in philosophical rather than political phrases. The president was attempting to become a moral leader, perhaps as Wilson did in 1918-1919. Wilson had failed; so would Hoover.

The Matter of Relief

Hoover saw in relief proposals a major threat to individual liberties. The drought would pass in time, he said, and when it did, the people in the area should be left with the feeling that they had helped themselves, that outside assistance had been marginal and in the form of loans and voluntary gifts. The dole was all right for Europe, but not America. And in Hoover's view, direct relief was a dole. If it were rejected, Americans would retain their self-respect and dignity; the national fabric would not have been rent or altered. In his State of the Union Message of December 3, 1930, Hoover took pride in the fact that "the local communities through their voluntary agencies have assumed the duty of relieving individual distress and are being generously supported by the public." In February he told reporters that "the basis of successful relief in national distress is to mobilize and organize the infinite number of agencies of self help in the community. That has been the American way of relieving distress . . ." Later in the month he spoke to the nation over radio on the issue:

> Victory over this depression and over other difficulties will be won by the resolution of our people to fight their own battles in their own communities, by stimulating their ingenuity to solve their own problems, by taking new courage to be masters of their own destiny in the struggle of life. This is not the easy way, but it is the American way.[14]

By then too, Hoover felt it necessary to defend himself against opposition charges of being heartless.

> I have indeed spent much of my life in fighting hardship and starvation both abroad and in the Southern states. I do not feel that I should be charged with lack of human sympathy for those who suffer, but I recall that in all the organizations with which I have been connected over these many years, the foundation has been to summon the maximum of self-help. I am proud to have sought the help of Congress in the past for nations who were so disorganized by war and anarchy that self-help was impossible. But even these appropriations were but a tithe of that which was coincidently mobilized from the public charity of the United States and foreign countries. There is no such paralysis in the United States and I am confident that our people have the resources, the initiative, the courage, the stamina and kindliness of spirit to meet this situation in the way they have met their problems over generations.[15]

The battle with Congress was joined. In the end $45 million was appropriated for farm aid, to be used by the Department of Agriculture for loans—not grants—to farmers for the purchase of seed, stock feed, fuel oil, and other farm necessities. In one draft some of the money was to be used for human food; Hoover strongly opposed this as being dangerously close to the dole. He noted that measures that would commit $4.5 billion had already been introduced by his opponents, and that most represented raids on the federal treasury. He had approved $150 million to enlarge public works programs, and considered this the limit to direct federal intervention at the time.[16]

Throughout the latter part of 1929 and all of 1930, Hoover had made optimistic statements to the press and public. "All the evidence indicates that the worst effect of the crash upon unemployment will have been passed during the next sixty days," he said on March 7, 1930. "Our joint undertaking has succeeded to a remarkable degree," Hoover added on May 1, concluding that "we have now passed the worst and with continued unity of effort we shall rapidly recover." In June he met a delegation asking for federal relief and told it all was going according to plan. "Gentlemen, you have come sixty days too late. The depression is over" (Document 7).[17]

Later on, such statements were quoted to show how little Hoover really understood the depression. In fact, there is more evidence to indicate Hoover said such things to bolster public confidence (Document 8). Unfortunately, he was not a sufficiently skillful politician to do this convincingly. Confidence in the nation, the economy, and the individual provided the subject matter for many of Hoover's speeches during the first year of the Great Depression. Increasingly, Hoover was losing confidence in himself. He fell into moods of deep gloom. "How I wish I could cheer up the poor old President and make him feel the importance of a little brightness and recreation in his own work," wrote Secretary of State Henry Stimson. "But after all I suppose he would reply and say that he gets his recreation in his own way and that my way would not suit him at all." Stimson wrote in his diary that an "ever present feeling of gloom . . . pervades everything connected with the Administration." On New Year's Eve he dropped by to wish Hoover a happy new year. The president "smiled one of his rather rare but sweet smiles and said, 'Well, it couldn't be any worse than this one anyhow.' "[18]

Later on, Hoover would claim that America was emerging from the depression in 1931 when European collapses struck the American economy with a new set of blows. These would lead to new responses, with additional powers assumed by the federal government. All the while Hoover would continue his defense of American individualism, warning the public not to surrender freedom for a mess of porridge. He failed, and the most popular American to emerge from World War I was transformed into the most reviled president since Andrew Johnson, while his successor—Franklin D. Roosevelt—was cheered as a hero. In 1938 Hoover ruefully remarked that he had been attacked for not ending the depression in three years, while Roosevelt was cheered although he had not brought prosperity after six years in office. He might have added, but did not, that Roosevelt was one of the most astute politicians the nation had ever produced, while he one of its poorest.

Hoover thought the American people would sacrifice all for liberty and freedom, learning these maxims not from direct experience in the nation, but acquiring them indirectly. He may have been wrong, or at least that would appear to have been the case in the early 1930s. Security, as much as freedom, was desired by the population. Hoover's way offered insufficient security in a world in which the corporate entities seemed to have control and the individual counted for less and less each year. "Progress will march if we hold an abiding faith in the intelligence, the initiative, the character, the courage, and the divine touch in the individual," wrote Hoover in 1922. "We can safeguard these ends if we give to each individual that opportunity for which the spirit of America stands. We can make a social system as perfect as our generation merits and one that will be received in gratitude by our children (Documents 9 and 10).[19]

Hoover never lost his faith, or his faith in the American people. But toward the end of the first year of the Great Depression, they had turned both from him and his reconstructed capitalist beliefs.

Notes

1. *Federal Reserve Bulletin,* September, 1929, p. 622.

2. The subject of the great securities craze of the 1920s, and in particular the stock market in 1929, has been the subject of many works, both scholarly and otherwise. Most take the view that speculation was rampant, government did not act to end abuses, and that the stock market was a good reflection of what has been characterized as a "decade of excess." It is also presented as a failure of capitalism. For this view, see John K. Galbraith, *The Great Crash* (Boston: Houghton Mifflin Co., 1955). A contrary interpretation may be found in Robert Sobel, *The Great Bull Market* (New York: Norton, 1968). The best study of the American economy in this period remains George Soule, *Prosperity Decade* (New York: Rinehart, 1947).

3. Arthur M. Schlesinger, Jr. *The Age of Roosevelt: The Crisis of the Old Order, 1919-1933* (Boston: Houghton Mifflin Co., 1957), pp. 162-63; Sobel, *Panic on Wall Street: A History of America's Financial Disasters* (New York: Macmillan, 1968), pp. 379-84.

4. In researches among "old timers" on Wall Street, the author has asked dozens of men whose careers began prior to World War I what their most vivid memory of business was. In no single instance did any say that Black Thursday was the worst day they could recall. Instead, most singled out the September 16, 1920 bombing of J.P. Morgan & Co. as their most frightening and memorable experience.

5. The banking crash took place in October, 1930, and in November alone, 256 banks suspended, while on December 11, the Bank of the United States, with over $200 million in deposits, closed its doors. Prior to October, however, deposits were higher than they had been in 1929. See Milton Friedman and Anna J. Schwartz, *A Monetary History of the United States, 1867-1960* (Princeton: Princeton University Press, 1963), pp. 308-9.

6. Edgerton spoke prior to the bank failures. In late 1930 the New York *World* ran a cartoon showing a man on a park bench talking to a squirrel. "But why didn't you save some money for the future, when times were good?" asked the squirrel. "I did," responded the victim of the bank failures. James W. Prothro, *The Dollar Decade: Business Ideas in the 1920s* (Baton Rouge: Louisiana State University Press, 1954), pp. 213-14.

7. Herbert C. Hoover, *Memoirs: The Great Depression,* (New York: Macmillian, 1951), pp. 30-31.

8. Schlesinger, *Crisis of the Old Order,* p. 226.

9. Hoover, *Memoirs: The Great Depression,* p. 4.

10. Herbert C. Hoover, *Memoirs: The Cabinet and the Presidency,* (New York: Macmillan, 1951), p. 298.

11. Jordan A. Schwarz, *The Interregnum of Despair: Hoover, Congress, and the Depression* (Urbana: University of Illinois Press, 1970), pp. 12-16.

12. *Business Week* called the program "a momentous experiment—the greatest since the war—in the possibilities of constructive cooperation between business and Government for the public protection and welfare." The New York *Times* said: "The President's course in this troublesome time has been all that could be desired. No one in his place could have done more; very few of his predecessors could have done as much." Albert V. Romasco, *The Poverty of Abundance: Hoover, the Nation, the Depression* (New York: Oxford University Press, 1965), pp. 35-36.

13. Schwarz, *Interregnum of Despair*, p. 17.

14. William Starr Myers, ed. *The State Papers and Other Writings of Herbert Hoover* (Garden City: Doubleday, Doran and Co., 1934), vol. I, pp. 500-5.

15. William Starr Myers and Walter H. Newton, *The Hoover Administration: A Documented Narrative* (New York: C. Scribner's Sons, 1936), p. 64.

16. The loan program was not a Hoover innovation. In 1922 Harding had supported an increase in loan activities, which was approved with Hoover's support. Robert K. Murray, *The Politics of Normalcy* (New York: 1973), p. 62.

17. Schlesinger, *Crisis of the Old Order*, pp. 165, 231.

18. Schwarz, *Interregnum of Despair*, pp. 50-51.

19. Herbert C. Hoover, *American Individualism* (Garden City: Doubleday, Page and Co., 1922), pp. 71-72.

part two

Documents of the Decision

1

"Shall We Have a Great Business Man as Chief Executive?"

Herbert Hoover was never a romantic figure, but in 1920 he appeared a man shrouded with the elements of romance. His world-wide engineering and business exploits, followed by his humanitarian work during World War I, made him appear both hardheaded and warmhearted. On many occasions he spoke feelingly of his belief in old-fashioned American values, while at the same time he represented the "engineering mind" and modernism. Thus, he combined the lure of the new with the stability of the old. It was little wonder, then, that both political parties considered him an excellent candidate for the presidency that year. Even after declining to run, Hoover remained a political force, the subject of many adulatory magazine and newspaper articles. The following, "Shall We Have A Great Business Man As Chief Executive?" is typical of this genre.

Document†
Both romance and success have been distinguishing characteristics of his career since, on graduating from Stanford, Hoover at the age of twenty-one, embarked for Australia as a mining engineer. Australian engineers, looking back twenty years, remember that the mine he chose to organize for production, and for which he raised capital, is the only property in its region that is still paying. It gave him an early reputation for good judgment and technical ability. With those assets he went to China to look over the undeveloped mineral resources of that empire. The Boxer trouble broke in his face and, we are told, wiped him out. When something like order was restored in the Celestial Empire he had nothing but certain concessions, valuable if they could be worked. With them he went to London, mining center for the world, and returned to China as junior partner in an old-established firm and, we read, the stockholders never had reason to regret the venture. Before he was forty this candidate for the American Presidency had explored interior China for metals, penetrating to places that had never seen a white face before. He had been wrecked on the China coast. He had served a machine gun in the siege of Tientsin. He had suppressed riots among Chinese coolie

†From: *Current Opinion* 68, no. 2 (May, 1920); 806-8.

gangs; he had stood for a whole night between these same workmen and the wrath of a German strafing party. He had trekked the veldt of South Africa, ridden the bush of Australia, traveled by droshky over the steppes of Siberia. Indeed the Muscovite Empire absorbed most of his main energies for two or three years—a proposition of opening up some iron properties which afterward grew into managing a principality. In the course of that job he was witness to an extraordinary gang murder and found himself tangled among the tragedies and comedies of the abortive first revolution. He had investigated in Asia Minor the old jewel mines of the Pharaohs, in the Alps the old iron mines of the Roman emperors. He had lain for weeks delirious with malarial fever somewhere in Burma.

His life, however, had not all been a wandering in far places. Other capitals of the world were almost as familiar to him as London. He was a figure in Shanghai, in Berlin, in Melbourne, in New York, in San Francisco. He must have traveled many times by P. & O. liner between London and Australia. On these long trips, says one biographer, he always took a secretary and a trunkful of papers, working all the way, rapidly transacting business by cable when the vessel touched at Suez or one of the Indian ports. In short, "he standardized his roving life, as he standardized the machinery of his companies. To judge from appearances, his acquaintances would say that he had worn that same double-breasted blue suit, the trousers slightly belled at the instep, for the past fifteen years. It always seems fresh and new, but it is apparently the same suit. That is because Hoover realized years ago how much time a man loses fiddling with clothes. Forthwith he left with his tailor a permanent order for one of those blue suits and for equally standard dress and dinner clothes. He laid similar orders with shirt maker and shoe dealer; just so, he standardized underclothes and accessories. During this roving period he kept rooms in Shanghai, New York, Melbourne, and San Francisco. In each of these he installed a set of his standardized clothes. Thereafter, whenever he arrived, all travel stained from steamer or Pullman, a fresh outfit of clothing was awaiting him. So he abated a nuisance which bothers every man who has outgrown his youthful vanities."

Those who have merely done business with him say they think of Hoover usually as a kindly but rather reserved person, going to the heart of a matter when he does speak but forming his sentences with deliberation. At dinner symposiums he is another person. He may sit silent for half an hour, listening, chuckling at the humorous sallies. Then something will stir recollection or observation and he will begin to talk until "the air seems full of light." The last two or three years before the war found him displaying his supreme talent—the organizing faculty. He has the art of taking complex forces and turning them into a working practical force. Called in at first as a specialist for sick properties, he has for long been in business a builder, not a juggler of profits, and at the time he was recommended to Ambassador Page to take charge of the Belgian relief work he was regarded by many as "the greatest mining engineer in the world." It was a very hard decision for Hoover to make. To abandon his large business interests, in that fantastic situation, would almost inevitably mean to lose whatever fortune he had accumulated and to begin life again at forty. But he "guessed he'd have to let the fortune go to blazes" and undertook the work which has made him an international figure and a candidate for the White House. As such, notes a writer in the New York *Sun,* he is developing strength, not as a man of magnetic qualities, but rather as one of exceptional business acumen, unusual capacity for concentrated effort, high ability as an executive and organizer and as a deep student of economic problems. That he studies deeply is evident from some things he has written. Often it is necessary to read him with the closest attention and sometimes to read him over again. His style suggests the somewhat ponderous phraseology of Grover Cleveland. As a writer of fluency, grace and striking expression he does not compare with President Wilson. In a recent magazine article, for instance, he employs a sentence of fifty-four words that does not contain a single punctuation mark, save the period, and it is almost impossible to get the full effect of that sentence without reading it a second or a third time. His aversion to writing—for it amounts to that—was romantically illustrated by the fact that his courtship, carried on between China, where he was then located, and Monterey, California, the home of Miss Lou Henry, was done by cable. She had been a "co-ed" at Leland Stanford when young Hoover was working his way through college, but it was not until the cable began working that the word marriage was flashed to her from the Orient and an acceptance was flashed back. A hurried trip from China to California and a quick ceremony followed.

Mrs. Hoover has been her husband's constant companion throughout his adventurous career. She went through the siege of Tientsin with him, living for six weeks behind barricades of rice bags and sugar barrels with death imminent every day. While Hoover helped man a machine gun, Mrs. Hoover served four-o'clock tea to the foreign colony. She is a strikingly beautiful woman and gracious hostess, still young—they were married in 1896. There are two small Hoovers, both boys. Their mother brought them over from London early in the war.

2

"American Individualism"

Hoover was perhaps the strongest secretary of commerce the nation had ever known. Not only did he enlarge upon the powers of his office, but he interested himself in the work of his fellow cabinet members, often to their chagrin. Finally, Hoover attempted to develop a philosophy of American individualism, first in a series of speeches in 1921-1922, then in a short book on the subject. Hoover's thoughts, a combination of old fashioned Social Darwinism, anti-Bolshevism, and technology, had great appeal for both conservatives and reformers in the 1920s, and earned Hoover a reputation as a political philosopher in government. One of the speeches, entitled "American Individualism," was written for a university commencement in 1922, and was reprinted in part in a leading magazine of the day.

Document†

Five or six great philosophies are at struggle in the world for ascendency. There is the Individualism of America. There is the Individualism of the more democratic states of Europe with its careful reservations of castes and classes. There are Communism, Socialism, Syndicalism, Capitalism, and finally there is Autocracy—whether by birth, land ownership, militarism, or divine right of kings—which still lingers on although our lifetime has seen fully two thirds of the earth's population, including Germany, Austria, Russia, and China, arrive at a state of angry disgust with this type of social motive power, and throw it on the scrap heap.

All those ideas are in ferment to-day in every country in the world. They fluctuate in ascendency with times and places. They compromise with each other in daily reaction on governments and peoples. Some of these ideas are perhaps more adapted to one race than another. Some are false, some are true. What we are interested in is their challenge to the physical and spiritual forces of America.

The partisans of some of these other brands of social schemes challenge us to comparison; and some of their partisans even among our own people are increasing in their agitation that we adopt one or another or parts of their devices in place of our tried individualism. They insist that our social foundations are exhausted, that like feudalism and autocracy America's plan has served its purpose—that it must be abandoned.

For myself, let me say at the very outset that my faith in the essential truth, strength and vitality of the developing creed by which we have hitherto lived in this country of ours, has been confirmed and deepened by the

†From: *World's Work* 43, no. 4 (April, 1922): 584-88. Reprinted by permission of the Herbert Hoover Foundation.

searching experiences in which I have shared. I am an individualist—an unashamed individualist—a proud individualist. But let me say also that I am an American individualist. It is not the individualism of other countries for which I would speak, but the individualism of America, with its profoundly developed character of abiding faith in the sovereign worth of individuality and its glorification of equality of opportunity for all.

We have a special social system of our own. We have made it ourselves; we have lived it; we have seldom tried to define it. It abhors autocracy and does not argue with it, but fights it. It is not capitalism or socialism or syndicalism. Like most Americans, I refuse to be damned by anybody's word-classification or to any kind of compartments that are based on the right of somebody dominating somebody else. The social force in which I am interested is far higher and far more precious a thing than all these. It springs from something infinitely more enduring; it springs from the one source of human progress—that each individual may be given the freedom for development of the best with which he has been endowed in heart and mind. There is no other source of progress.

Individualism has been the primary force of American civilization for three centuries. It is individualism that has supplied the motivation of America's political, economic, and spiritual institutions in all these years. Our very form of government is the product of the individualism of our people, the demand for an equal opportunity, for a fair chance. Democracy is merely the mechanism which individualism invented as a device that would carry on the necessary political work of social organization, with the minimum of interference with economic and spiritual individualism. Democracy arises out of individualism and alone prospers through it.

The American pioneer is the epic expression of that individualism and the pioneer spirit of response to the challenge of opportunity, to the challenge of nature, to the challenge of life, to the call of the frontier. That spirit need never die for lack of something for it to achieve. There will always be a frontier to conquer or to hold as long as men think and plan and dare. Our American individualism has received much of its character from our contacts with the forces of nature on a new continent. The days of the pioneer are not over. The great continent of science is as yet explored only on its borders, and it is only the pioneer who will penetrate the frontier in the quest for new worlds to conquer. The very genius of our institutions has been given to them by the pioneer spirit. Our individualism is rooted in our very nature. It is based on conviction born of experience. Equal opportunity, the demand for a fair chance, became the formula of American individualism because it was the method of American achievement. . . .

3-a ════════

═════════ "Herbert Hoover
and the
Republican
Party"

By the early summer of 1928 it appeared evident that Hoover would become the Republican presidential nominee, and then go on to win in November. What kind of president would he be? Reformers and conservatives alike viewed him as representative of a new force in presidential politics—a reformer from without the progressive reform tradition, and a conservative who was willing to innovate. The idea of a Hoover presidency excited and troubled both political factions.

The *New Republic*, a progressive journal founded by Wilsonians, had been more interested in foreign policy than domestic concerns in the 1920s. Yet it had been critical of both Harding and Coolidge, while praising Hoover. In 1928 the journal hailed the coming Hoover presidency, while voicing doubts as to its effectiveness that turned out to be most accurate.

Document†

IN NOMINATING Herbert Hoover for the presidency, the Republicans have entrusted the responsibility of leadership to the member of their party who is best prepared for the work. He is not the most popular candidate whom they could have named. He will not, if elected, arrange for the party and the country an administration as neutral and as non-contentious as that of Mr. Coolidge. As nominee and as President, Mr. Hoover's career is likely to be controversial, agitated and not scrupulously considerate of partisan Republican susceptibilities. Yet from the point of view of the welfare of the Republican party in its relation to the welfare of the country, Mr. Hoover is more likely than any other Republican who could have been named both to fertilize the one promising motive in the party's life and to minimize its sterile tendency toward mere inertia which Mr. Coolidge has so conscientiously rationalized. He represents the only vital ingredient in Republicanism which may serve as a positive leaven in the future conduct and policy of the party.

Mr. Hoover believes in the subordination of government to business, and is in this essential respect an orthodox Republican. He envisages the United States as a society of free individuals who enjoy essential equality of economic opportunity and who, in severally pursuing their own welfare, are contributing effectively to the collective welfare. Americans of all classes, from his point of view,

†From: "Herbert Hoover and the Republican Party," *New Republic* 55 (June 27, 1928): 133-5. Reprinted by permission of *The New Republic,* ©1928, Harrison-Blaine of New Jersey.

are worthily occupied in seeking their personal interests, and for the most part and wherever possible, they ought to be let alone. It is only through the successful carrying on of these private economic activities that American society can yield the largest possible sum of general fulfillment. The individuals who carry them on successfully are the chief benefactors of society, and if the government seeks, in addition to keeping order, to promote social welfare, it must undertake the job in coöperation with successful business men or in subordination to them. The function of government in relation to business is to safeguard its essential interests, to respect its essential purposes and even to encourage its essential activities. In his belief in all these doctrines Mr. Hoover is a sound Republican and a belated adherent of the pioneer tradition. That is what he means when he announces and reaffirms his loyal adhesion to Coolidgism.

While, however, he believes in the subordination of government to business, he believes also in the subordination of both government and business to another sovereign whose authority was not recognized in the day of the pioneer. The new sovereign is not as yet crowned with any title and his kingdom is not exercised by means of laws and orders, but it is a kingdom of this world and neither business nor government can escape its authority. Let us call it for the moment scientific method in its application to the pursuit of human ends. The introduction of this new secular god into the American pantheon is bound to exercise a disconcerting effect on the kind of allegiance which is granted to the two older gods of American practice. The people who believed in business as the salutary activity to which government should be subordinated, and those who believed in government as the salutary activity to which business should be subordinated have accepted the purposes of business or government at their advertised value and transferred this value from the object of the activity to its result. Pioneer Americanism assumed incautiously that if the individuals who make up a free society were encouraged to pursue their personal economic welfare, they would combine to achieve happiness for the whole group. The social democrat has assumed with a similar lack of caution the necessity of interference with this individual scramble for power and wealth, the hopelessness of achieving social welfare except by virtue of social motives and the technical competence of government to serve these public objects. But a citizen who bestows his allegiance on scientific method is concerned primarily about the fruits of an activity and only secondarily about its object. His attention is fastened on the processes which are supposed to lead to an admirable consummation rather than on the announced and sanctified goal itself. The priests of the new religion of scientific method are occupied with question marks about the outcome of activities rather than with conclusions about their values.

Herbert Hoover's emphasis on method implies, consequently, the introduction of a distracting element into the Coolidge-Republican Utopia. It is very well to believe in business and to subordinate government to it, but those who put their trust in scientific method are obliged to question whether rule-of-thumb business is capable of achieving its alleged objects. During his career as Secretary of Commerce Mr. Hoover has labored to improve the older methods of conducting business. He has tried to identify the function of government in relation thereto with the introduction of more efficient methods into economic processes. He has hoped in this way to strengthen the operation of the Republican economy without raising any question about the existing distribution of economic power and without invoking political agitation. The great majority of the influential business men of the country approved of his program, and with their help he has sold it to the Republican party. After having nominated him as its candidate for President, the party has for the moment taken it over. He has indicated the only constructive direction in which the Republican party can move, and he is to be congratulated upon seizing it, upon recruiting a certain amount of support for it among business men and in getting himself nominated as its representative in politics.

But it is a poor omen of a prosperous candidacy or presidency for Mr. Hoover that the Republican party, after having nominated him on his merits as a man and as a leader, shows very little enthusiasm for its own handiwork. Its suppressed uneasiness and irritation justify the prediction of a perilous career for Mr. Hoover as candidate, and, if elected, either a stormy or a compromising career as President. The Republican politicians are far from being converted to the subordination of politics to engineering method. They have accepted Mr. Hoover as the representative of the most energetic and capable element in American practical affairs, but they will not allow him to ride them very hard without balking; and if subsequently he gets involved in conflict with them, his own shortcomings as a popular leader will handicap him severely. Doubtless his leadership will pass unchallenged during the campaign (which will be conducted on the basis of substituting organization for popular emotional appeal), but should he be elected, he will, in order to lead the Republican politicians anywhere, have to quarrel with a great many of them. He will have to work with a party which is united only in defending vested interests and privileges. Any attempt to formulate and carry out a positive policy of any kind will breed acute dissensions among Republicans of different classes, sections and opinions.

Even more serious for Mr. Hoover, however, would be an effort on his part to translate into political terms his program of business efficiency. As Secretary of Commerce he has helped business men to conduct their existing affairs more methodically and successfully—that is, to increase output, to lower production costs and to coöperate more effectively in manufacturing and marketing their products. But he has assumed little or no responsibility for any improvement in business method which was not quickly and demonstrably profitable to individual business men. They have worked with him on that assumption, and as the clerk of President Coolidge, he did not need to ask for anything different or more inclusive. He could shift to the back of his chief the responsibility for initiating or not initiating economic policies which were not and could not be justified by an immediately increased profit. But as President he would have to assume responsibility for increasing the efficiency of business in respects which do not interest business men as individual producers and which may involve expenditures and sacrifices on their part. He will have to tackle the problems of applying his engineering methods to the more flimsy parts of the economic structure—to the agrarian depression, to unemployment, to the concentration of electric power in a few hands without effective public control, to the disorganized coal industry and to the unsatisfactory relationship between organized industry and organized labor. If his attitude toward these questions is as evasive and complacent as that of President Coolidge, the progressive opinion of the country will size up his proposed application of scientific method to economic processes as merely a hypocritical attempt to rationalize Mellonism, and will cease to cherish any hopes or illusions about him. On the other hand, if he really tries to introduce into economic processes improvements which are more interesting to wage-earners, farmers and consumers than they are to financiers and business executives, he will soon find himself engaged in a fierce quarrel with his own party.

The dilemma is real, and when Mr. Hoover seeks to extricate himself from it he will do so at a heavy cost of some kind. His easiest way out would undoubtedly be to follow faithfully in Mr. Coolidge's footsteps and to immerse the grave national problems of economic adjustment in a cloud of weasel words. But Mr. Hoover is not like that. He brings an active and a realistic intelligence to the examination of concrete problems, and his personal instincts demand of him decisions rather than pretentious and evasive discourse. His mind is occupied with the study of processes and the effort to improve them rather than with the elaboration of principles and the justification of conclusions. He honestly wishes to combine progressivism with conservatism, and he could not as President sell his conscience by accepting payment in Coolidge currency without cheapening himself in his own eyes. During the campaign he will have to squirm, for, while he can decide nothing until he is President, he will be obliged as a candidate to discourse about everything, and he cannot in what he says take many liberties with Coolidge doctrine. The concentration of the LaFollette, the agrarian and labor union vote on Smith may, consequently, defeat him. If he should pull through the severe test of the election, he will have a breathing spell. During the first few months a President is always right. When his new troubles come, he will, moreover, be better armed with the powers and opportunities of his office to deal with them. But come they soon will, chiefly from the insubordinate and irreconcilable elements in his own party, and he will need magnanimity as well as adroitness and determination to deal with them. He will put up a valiant but probably in the end an unsuccessful fight. The inertia of the Republican politicians and the unintelligence of American business men in relation to public affairs will wear him out. He will be unable to recruit the following with which successfully to oppose them, and he will in the end either conform or quit. But he would, we hope, have started something which as a fermenting influence in American politics will survive, even if it has to be abandoned by the man who started it.

3-b

A Speech from Candidate Hoover

During the 1928 presidential campaign Hoover further enunciated his philosophy of government and attempted to place it in a historical context. In his speeches he made it clear he meant to be an activist president, to bring his philosophy of government and government-business relations to the White House in a vigorous fashion. As before, he would retain traditional American values while wedding them to the new technology of the post-World War I world.

The following speech was delivered in New York on October 22, 1928.

Document†

"You cannot extend the mastery of the government over the daily working life of a people without at the same time making it the master of the people's souls and thoughts. Every expansion of government in business means that government in order to protect itself from the political consequences of its errors and wrongs is driven irresistibly without peace to greater and greater control of the nation's press and platform. Free speech does not live many hours after free industry and free commerce die."

"It is a false liberalism that interprets itself into the government operation of commercial business. Every step of bureaucratizing of the business of our country poisons the very roots of liberalism—that is, political equality, free speech, free assembly, free press, and equality of opportunity. It is the road not to more liberty, but to less liberty. Liberalism should be found not striving to spread bureaucracy but striving to set bounds to it. True liberalism seeks all legitimate freedom first in the confident belief that without such freedom the pursuit of all other blessings and benefits is vain. That belief is the foundation of all American progress, political as well as economic."

"Liberalism is a force truly of the spirit, a force proceeding from the realization that economic freedom cannot be sacrificed if political freedom is to be preserved. Even if governmental conduct of business could give us more efficiency instead of less efficiency, the fundamental objection to it would remain unaltered and unabated. It would destroy political equality. It would increase rather than decrease abuse and corruption. It would stifle initiative and invention. It would undermine the development of leadership. It would

†From: Herbert Hoover, *The New Day, Campaign Speeches of Herbert Hoover, 1928* (Stanford: Stanford University Press, 1928), pp. 162-64. Quoted by authorization of the Herbert Hoover Foundation.

cramp and cripple the mental and spiritual energies of our people. It would extinguish equality and opportunity. It would dry up the spirit of liberty and progress. For these reasons primarily it must be resisted. For a hundred and fifty years liberalism has found its true spirit in the American System, not in the European systems."

"I do not wish to be misunderstood in this statement. I am defining a general policy. It does not mean that our government is to part with one iota of its natural resources without complete protection to the public interest."

"Nor do I wish to be misinterpreted as believing that the United States is free-for-all and devil-take-the-hindmost. The very essence of equality of opportunity and of American individualism is that there shall be no domination by any group or combination in this republic, whether it be business or political. On the contrary, it demands economic justice as well as political and social justice. It is no system of *laissez faire*."

"I feel deeply on this subject because during the war I had some practical experience with governmental operation and control. I have witnessed not only at home but abroad the many failures of government in business. I have seen its tyrannies, its injustices, its destructions of self-government, its undermining of the very instincts which carry our people forward to progress. I have witnessed the lack of advance, the lowered standards of living, the depressed spirits of people working under such a system. My objection is based not upon theory or upon a failure to recognize wrong or abuse, but I know the adoption of such methods would strike at the very roots of American life and would destroy the very basis of American progress."

"Our people have the right to know whether we can continue to solve our great problems without abandonment of our American System. I know we can. We have demonstrated that our system is responsive enough to meet any new and intricate development in our economic and business life. We have demonstrated that we can meet any economic problem and still maintain our democracy as master in its own house, and that we can at the same time preserve equality of opportunity and individual freedom."

"In the last fifty years we have discovered that mass production will produce articles for us at half the cost they required previously. We have seen the resultant growth of large units of production and distribution. This is big business. Many businesses must be bigger, for our tools are bigger, our country is bigger. We now build a single dynamo of a hundred thousand horsepower. Even fifteen years ago that would have been a big business all by itself. Yet today advance in production requires that we set ten of these units together in a row."

"The American people from bitter experience have a rightful fear that great business units might be used to dominate our industrial life and by illegal and unethical practices destroy equality of opportunity."

"Years ago the Republican administration established the principle that such evils could be corrected by regulation. It developed methods by which abuses could be prevented while the full value of industrial progress could be retained for the public. It insisted upon the principle that when great public utilities were clothed with the security of partial monopoly, whether it be railways, power plants, telephones, or what not, then there must be the fullest and most complete control of rates, services, and finances by government or local agencies. It declared that these businesses must be conducted with glass pockets."

"As to our great manufacturing and distributing industries, the Republican Party insisted upon the enactment of laws that not only would maintain competition, but would destroy conspiracies to destroy the smaller units or dominate and limit the equality of opportunity amongst our people."

"One of the great problems of government is to determine to what extent the government shall regulate and control commerce and industry and how much it shall leave it alone. No system is perfect. We have had many abuses in the private conduct of business. That every good citizen resents. It is just as important that business keep out of government as that government keep out of business.

"Nor am I setting up the contention that our institutions are perfect. No human ideal is ever perfectly attained, since humanity itself is not perfect."

4

Inaugural Address

In his writings and speeches during the 1920s Hoover strove for clarity rather than eloquence, perhaps because he had little talent for the latter. In his Inaugural Address of March 4, 1929, he indicated that in his view, the nation's major problems were failures in the system of criminal justice, enforcement of prohibition, education, public health, and the relation of government to business. As for the future, Hoover thought it was bright. Although he was worried about weaknesses in the economy and speculation on Wall Street, he did not mention them at that time.

As was the case with most other inaugural addresses, Hoover ended his on notes of hope.

Document†

. . . .It appears to me that the more important further mandates from the recent election were the maintenance of the integrity of the Constitution; the vigorous enforcement of the laws; the continuance of economy in public expenditure; the continued regulation of business to prevent domination in the community; the denial of ownership or operation of business by the Government in competition with its citizens; the avoidance of policies which would involve us in the controversies of foreign nations; the more effective reorganization of the departments of the Federal Government; the expansion of public works; and the promotion of welfare activities affecting education and the home.

These were the more tangible determinations of the election, but beyond them was the confidence and belief of the people that we would not neglect the support of the embedded ideals and aspirations of America. These ideals and aspirations are the touchstones upon which the day-to-day administration and legislative acts of government must be tested. More than this, the Government must, so far as lies within its proper powers, give leadership to the realization of these ideals and to the fruition of these aspirations. No one can adequately reduce these things of the spirit to phrases or to a catalogue of definitions. We do know what the attainments of these ideals should be: The preservation of self-government and its full foundations in local government; the perfection of justice whether in economic or in social fields; the maintenance of ordered liberty; the denial of domination by any group or

†From: U. S. Congress, House *Inaugural Addresses of the Presidents of the United States,* 91 Cong., 1st Sess., 1969, pp. 225-33.

class; the building up and preservation of equality of opportunity; the stimulation of initiative and individuality; absolute integrity in public affairs; the choice of officials for fitness to office; the direction of economic progress toward prosperity for the further lessening of poverty; the freedom of public opinion; the sustaining of education and of the advancement of knowledge; the growth of religious spirit and the tolerance of all faiths; the strenghtening of the home; the advancement of peace.

There is no short road to the realization of these aspirations. Ours is a progressive people, but with a determination that progress must be based upon the foundation of experience. Ill-considered remedies for our faults bring only penalties after them. But if we hold the faith of the men in our mighty past who created these ideals, we shall leave them heightened and strengthened for our children.

This is not the time and place for extended discussion. The questions before our country are problems of progress to higher standards; they are not the problems of degeneration. They demand thought and they serve to quicken the conscience and enlist our sense of responsibility for their settlement. And that responsibility rests upon you, my countrymen, as much as upon those of us who have been selected for office.

Ours is a land rich in resources; stimulating in its glorious beauty; filled with millions of happy homes; blessed with comfort and opportunity. In no nation are the institutions of progress more advanced. In no nation are the fruits of accomplishment more secure. In no nation is the government more worthy of respect. No country is more loved by its people. I have an abiding faith in their capacity, integrity and high purpose. I have no fears for the future of our country. It is bright with hope.

In the presence of my countrymen, mindful of the solemnity of this occasion, knowing what the task means and the responsibility which it involves, I beg your tolerance, your aid, and your cooperation. I ask the help of Almighty God in this service to my country to which you have called me.

5

Hoover's Message to the Special Session of Congress, April, 1929

Shortly after entering the White House Hoover called a special session of Congress to deal with agricultural distress and the tariff, which he saw as interrelated problems. At the time it appeared the nation would remain prosperous, and that strong supportive measures would be needed only in these two areas. Although the situation changed by the end of the year, Hoover continued to consider his message to the special session on April 16, 1929, a key document in the recovery effort, and he wavered little from its content or spirit. For this reason, it is one of the more significant statements of the early period of the depression.

Document†
Message to the First Session of the Seventy-first Congress, *April 16, 1929.* Special Session for Farm Relief and Limited Changes in the Tariff.

To the Congress of the United States:
I have called this special session of Congress to redeem two pledges given in the last election—farm relief and limited changes in the tariff.

The difficulties of the agricultural industry arise out of a multitude of causes. A heavy indebtedness was inherited by the industry from the deflation processes of 1920. Disorderly and wasteful methods of marketing have developed. The growing specialization in the industry has for years been increasing the proportion of products that now leave the farm and, in consequence, prices have been unduly depressed by congested marketing at the harvest or by the occasional climatic surpluses. Railway rates have necessarily increased. There has been a growth of competition in the world markets from countries that enjoy cheaper labor or more nearly virgin soils. There was a great expansion of production from our marginal lands during the war, and upon these profitable enterprise under normal conditions can not be maintained. Meanwhile their continued output tends to aggravate the

†From: William Starr Myers, ed., *The State Papers and Other Public Writings of Herbert Hoover* (Garden City: Doubleday, Doran and Co., 1934), pp. 31-37. Reprinted by permission of the Herbert Hoover Foundation.

situation. Local taxes have doubled and in some cases trebled. Work animals have been steadily replaced by mechanical appliances, thereby decreasing the consumption of farm products. There are many other contributing causes.

The general result has been that our agricultural industry has not kept pace in prosperity or standards of living with other lines of industry.

There being no disagreement as to the need of farm relief, the problem before us becomes one of method by which relief may be most successfully brought about. Because of the multitude of causes and because agriculture is not one industry but a score of industries, we are confronted not with a single problem alone but a great number of problems. Therefore there is no single plan or principle that can be generally applied. Some of the forces working to the detriment of agriculture can be greatly mitigated by improving our waterway transportation; some of them by readjustment of the tariff; some by better understanding and adjustment of production needs; and some by improvement in the methods of marketing.

An effective tariff upon agricultural products, that will compensate the farmer's higher costs and higher standards of living, has a dual purpose. Such a tariff not only protects the farmer in our domestic market but it also stimulates him to diversify his crops and to grow products that he could not otherwise produce, and thus lessens his dependence upon exports to foreign markets. The great expansion of production abroad under the conditions I have mentioned renders foreign competition in our export markets increasingly serious. It seems but natural, therefore, that the American farmer, having been greatly handicapped in his foreign market by such competition from the younger expanding countries, should ask that foreign access to our domestic market should be regulated by taking into account the differences in our costs of production.

The Government has a special mandate from the recent election, not only to further develop our waterways and revise the agricultural tariff, but also to extend systematic relief in other directions.

I have long held that the multiplicity of causes of agricultural depression could only be met by the creation of a great instrumentality clothed with sufficient authority and resources to assist our farmers to meet these problems, each upon its own merits. The creation of such an agency would at once transfer the agricultural question from the field of politics into the realm of economics and would result in constructive action. The administration is pledged to create an instrumentality that will investigate the causes, find sound remedies, and have the authority and resources to apply those remedies.

The pledged purpose of such a Federal farm board is the reorganization of the marketing system on sounder and more stable and more economic lines. To do this the board will require funds to assist in creating and sustaining farmer-owned and farmer-controlled agencies for a variety of purposes, such as the acquisition of adequate warehousing and other facilities for marketing; adequate working capital to be advanced against commodities lodged for storage; necessary and prudent advances to corporations created and owned by farmers' marketing organizations for the purchase and orderly marketing of surpluses occasioned by climatic variations or by harvest congestion; to authorize the creation and support of clearing houses, especially for perishable products, through which, under producers' approval, coöperation can be established with distributors and processors to more orderly marketing of commodities and for the elimination of many wastes in distribution; and to provide for licensing of handlers of some perishable products so as to eliminate unfair practices. Every penny of waste between farmer and consumer that we can eliminate, whether it arises from methods of distribution or from hazard or speculation, will be a gain to both farmer and consumer.

In addition to these special provisions in the direction of improved returns, the board should be organized to investigate every field of economic betterment for the farmer so as to furnish guidance as to need in production, to devise methods for elimination of unprofitable marginal lands and their adaptation to other uses; to develop industrial by-products and to survey a score of other fields of helpfulness.

Certain safeguards must naturally surround these activities and the instrumentalities that are created. Certain vital principles must be adhered to in order that we may not undermine the freedom of our farmers and of our people as a whole by bureaucratic and governmental domination and interference. We must not undermine initiative. There should be no fee or tax imposed upon the farmer. No governmental agency should engage in the buying and selling and price fixing of products, for such courses can lead only to bureaucracy and domination. Government funds should not be loaned or facilities duplicated where other services of credit and facilities are available at reasonable rates. No activities should be set in motion that will result in increasing the surplus production, as such will defeat any plans of relief.

The most progressive movement in all agriculture has been the upbuilding of the farmer's own marketing organizations, which now embrace nearly two million farmers in membership and annually distribute nearly $2,500,000,000 worth of farm products. These organizations have acquired experience in virtually every branch of their industry, and furnish a substantial basis upon which to build further organization. Not all these marketing organizations are of the same type, but the test of them is whether or not they are farmer owned or farmer controlled. In order to strengthen and not to undermine them, all proposals for governmental assistance should originate with such organizations and be the result of their application. Moreover, by such bases of organization the Government will be removed from engaging in the business of agriculture.

The difficulties of agriculture can not be cured in a day; they can not all be cured by legislation; they can not be cured by the Federal Government alone. But farmers and their organizations can be assisted to overcome these inequalities. Every effort of this character is an experiment, and we shall find from our experience the way to further advance. We must make a start. With the creation of a great instrumentality of this character, of a strength and importance equal to that of those which we have created for transportation and banking, we give immediate assurance of the determined purpose of the Government to meet the difficulties of which we are now aware, and to create an agency through which constructive action for the future will be assured.

In this treatment of this problem we recognize the responsibility of the people as a whole, and we shall lay the foundations for a new day in agriculture, from which we shall preserve to the Nation the great values of its individuality and strengthen our whole national fabric.

In considering the tariff for other industries than agriculture, we find that there have been economic shifts necessitating a readjustment of some of the tariff schedules. Seven years of experience under the tariff bill enacted in 1922 have demonstrated the wisdom of Congress in the enactment of that measure. On the whole it has worked well. In the main our wages have been maintained at high levels; our exports and imports have steadily increased; with some exceptions our manufacturing industries have been prosperous. Nevertheless, economic changes have taken place during that time, which have placed certain domestic products at a disadvantage and new industries have come into being, all of which creates the necessity for some limited changes in the schedules and in the administrative clauses of the laws as written in 1922.

It would seem to me that the test of necessity for revision is in the main whether there has been a substantial slackening of activity in an industry during the past few years, and a consequent decrease of employment due to insurmountable competition in the products of that industry. It is not as if we were setting up a new basis of protective duties. We did that seven years ago. What we need to remedy now is whatever substantial loss of employment may have resulted from shifts since that time.

No discrimination against any foreign industry is involved in equalizing the difference in costs of production at home and abroad and thus taking from foreign producers the advantages they derive from paying lower wages to labor. Indeed, such equalization is not only a measure of social justice at home, but by the lift it gives to our standards of living we increase the demand for those goods from abroad that we do not ourselves produce. In a large sense we have learned that the cheapening of the toiler decreases rather than promotes permanent prosperity because it reduces the consuming power of the people.

In determining changes in our tariff we must not fail to take into account the broad interests of the country as a whole, and such interests include our trade relations with other countries. It is obviously unwise protection which sacrifices a greater amount of employment in exports to gain a less amount of employment from imports.

I am impressed with the fact that we also need important revision in some of the administrative phases of the tariff. The Tariff Commission should be reorganized and placed upon a basis of higher salaries in order that we may at all times command men of the broadest attainments. Seven years of experience have proved the principle of flexible tariff to be practical, and in the long view a most important principle to maintain. However, the basis upon which the Tariff Commission makes its recommendations to the President for administrative changes in the rates of duty should be made more automatic and more comprehensive, to the end that the time required for determinations by the Tariff Commission shall be greatly shortened. The formula upon which the commission must now act often requires that years be consumed in reaching conclusions where it should require only months. Its very purpose is defeated by delays. I believe a formula can be found that will insure rapid and accurate determination of needed changes in rates. With such strengthening of the Tariff Commission and of its basis for action many secondary changes in tariff can well be left to action by the commission, which at the same time will give complete security to industry for the future.

Furthermore, considerable weaknesses on the administrative side of the tariff have developed, especially in the valuations for assessments of duty. There are cases of undervaluations that are difficult to discover without access to the books of foreign manufacturers, which they are reluctant to offer. This has become also a great source of friction abroad. There is increasing shipment of goods on consignment, particularly by foreign shippers to concerns that they control in the United States, and this practice makes valuations difficult to determine. I believe it is desirable to furnish to the Treasury a sounder basis for valuation in these and other cases.

It is my understanding that it is the purpose of the leaders of Congress to confine the deliberations of the session mainly to the questions of farm relief and tariff. In this policy I concur. There are, however, certain matters of emergency legislation that were partially completed in the last session, such as the decennial census, the reapportionment of congressional representation, and the suspension of the national-origins clause of the immigration act of 1924, together with some minor administrative authorizations. I understand that these measures can be reundertaken without unduly extending the session. I recommended their consummation as being in the public interest.

HERBERT HOOVER.

The White House,
April 16, 1929.

6

"The Causes and Course of the Depression"

Writing in 1937, Hoover's close friends and former members of his cabinet, Ray Wilbur (secretary of the interior) and Arthur Hyde (secretary of agriculture) presented the Hoover view of the causes of the depression and the methods employed to alleviate its impact and bring it to a close. Their picture was one of an active leader expanding upon presidential powers, concerned with the population's well-being, prepared with a program that would end the distress and preserve basic liberties at the same time.

Document†

The Causes and Course of the Depression

The origins and the progress of the depression largely determined the policies required to combat it.

Its origins lay in the World War and it was world wide. The destruction of 20,000,000 lives, of hundreds of billions of property, the creation of 200 billion dollar governmental debts, the inflated expansion of certain industries, including agriculture, the uneconomic boundaries of the Peace Treaties, the unbalanced budgets, the fugitive flight of capital from one country to another seeking safety, and the constant inflations of credit and currency over the world in attempts to stand off the evil day of liquidation—all piled up a flood that had to burst.

There were immediate causes in the United States which contributed to precipitate and to intensify the crash. After the war Presidents Harding and Coolidge had prudently balanced the budget, reduced the debt and we were slowly liquidating our war losses and rebuilding a great prosperity on the sole basis of increasing national efficiency. But the United States also, in 1927, started credit inflation on the mistaken notion of our Federal Reserve leaders that we could help to tide over a threatening European slackening of business. Out of this inflation and other causes, including too much optimism and failure to pass on decreasing costs to the consumer, the United States was enveloped in a period of mad speculation which crashed in October, 1929.

†From: Ray Lyman Wilbur and Arthur Mastick Hyde, *The Hoover Policies* (New York: C. Scribner's Sons, 1937), pp. 359-62. Reprinted by permission of Charles Scribner's Sons from *The Hoover Policies* by Ray Lyman Wilbur and Arthur Mastick Hyde. Copyright 1937 Charles Scribner's Sons.

Hoover as Secretary of Commerce had made repeated protests against these Federal Reserve Board policies and repeated warnings against the wild speculation. At the first proposal of these policies he had protested, "The Reserve policies . . . mean inflation with inevitable collapse which will bring calamities upon our farmers, our workers and legitimate business." We may quote his statements on the rise of speculation at various times, "The . . . safety of continued prosperity will depend on . . . caution and resistance to . . . speculation . . . our bankers can check the dangers of speculative credits. . . ." "The real test . . . will be whether we can hold this . . . prosperity without . . . an era of speculation and extravagance with its inevitable debacle. . . ." "Unless our financial policies are guided with courage and wisdom this speculation . . . can only land us on the shores of depression. . . . Not since 1920 have we required . . . a more capable administration of credit facilities than now. . . ."

When Hoover became President he inherited three things: first, a crazy speculative boom in the United States; second, a hidden impending European financial collapse; and third, a weak and badly organized banking system.

It is necessary to remember that depressions are the retribution of previous economic follies and wrong-doings and not the cause of them. It is obvious that, when they break, the inflationary and speculative values must be liquidated down to realities. Time is required for such readjustments, both in values of stocks, real estate, fictitiously high commodities and in the fictitious debts founded upon them. Further, the waste, bad management and extravagance in industry incident to booms and speculation must be eliminated. But of equal importance, the minds of individual citizens and of the nation must be adjusted to better moral standards and the change to a less extravagant form of life than those which existed in the boom. Again boom periods are always the scene of extra wrong-doing and villainy. And the depression brings about the exposure of accumulated weaknesses in the economic system which must be met by great economic and social reforms.

The movements of the depression and recovery during the Hoover Administration divide themselves into four definite periods, each requiring adaptations of policies and methods.

The first period of eighteen months extended from the market crash in October, 1929, while the United States and the rest of the world were liquidating their inflated stock and business boom. Had that been all there was to it, our beginnings of recovery in early 1931 would have lifted us out of it and it would have been but an episode, not dangerous to our civilization. . . .

Hoover's first, and in fact revolutionary, policy in handling the depression was to hold that the Federal Government had an obligation to perform in mitigating the effects of the depression and expediting recovery. Never before in a score of depressions, some almost as severe, had any President taken any part or used any of the strength of the Federal Government in such a battle in behalf of the people.

The dominant Hoover policies were:

1. To stimulate and organize the people to themselves take co-operative action in every direction to meet the problems of the depression.
2. To insist on the full action of local and state governments.
3. When such action was insufficient then to bring the full strength of the Federal Government behind the people's organizations and their local and state governments.

Under these dominant policies, the President set up these principal lines of Federal action.

a. To provide against suffering from hunger and cold among the dislocated and unemployed, by staggering employment, by increased construction work and by relief.

b. To cushion the inevitable downward readjustments of wages and farm prices which inevitably must recede from boom levels.

c. To secure co-operation between employers and employees which would preserve the country from industrial conflicts and the social disorder which had usually arisen in depression.

d. To preserve sound currency, to secure, if possible, from Congress a balanced budget as the very bulwark of National credit.

e. To buttress the credit institutions of the country so as to prevent panic and business bankruptcy and the widespread dispossession of homes and farms.

f. To co-operate with other nations in remedying the world-wide forces of the depression.

g. To build fundamental reforms in business and banking but, where these reforms would dislocate recovery, then to suspend reform for the greater purpose of returning people to work.

h. To sustain the courage of the people.

i. To hold rigidly to the Constitution and the liberties of the people under any stress that might arise.

7

Message to Congress: December, 1930

In his second annual message to Congress on December 2, 1930, Hoover reviewed the efforts of his administration in meeting the depression during its first year. He clearly believed the depression was on its way to being corrected, and that his policies were proving effective. Thus, he asked for no new measures from Congress, and wrote in a self-congratulatory fashion.

Document†

To the Senate and House of Representatives:

I have the honor to comply with the requirement of the Constitution that I should lay before the Congress information as to the state of the Union, and recommend consideration of such measures as are necessary and expedient.

Substantial progress has been made during the year in national peace and security; the fundamental strength of the Nation's economic life is unimpaired; education and scientific discovery have made advances; our country is more alive to its problems of moral and spiritual welfare.

Economic Situation During the past 12 months we have suffered with other nations from economic depression.

The origins of this depression lie to some extent within our own borders through a speculative period which diverted capital and energy into speculation rather than constructive enterprise. Had overspeculation in securities been the only force operating, we should have seen recovery many months ago, as these particular dislocations have generally readjusted themselves.

Other deep-seated causes have been in action, however, chiefly the world-wide overproduction beyond even the demand of prosperous times for such important basic commodities as wheat, rubber, coffee, sugar, copper, silver, zinc, to some extent cotton, and other raw materials. The cumulative effects of demoralizing price falls of these important commodities in the process of adjustment of production to world consumption have produced financial crises in many countries and have diminished the buying power of these countries for imported goods to a degree which extended the difficulties farther afield by creating unemployment in all the industrial

†From: New York *Times*, December 3, 1930. ©1930 by The New York Times Company. Reprinted by permission.

nations. The political agitation in Asia; revolutions in South America and political unrest in some European States; the methods of sale by Russia of her increasing agricultural exports to European markets; and our own drought— have all contributed to prolong and deepen the depression.

In the larger view the major forces of the depression now lie outside of the United States, and our recuperation has been retarded by the unwarranted degree of fear and apprehension created by these outside forces.

The extent of the depression is indicated by the following approximate percentages of activity during the past three months as compared with the highly prosperous year of 1928:

Value of department-store sales . . . . 93% of 1928

Volume of manufacturing production . . . . 80% of 1928

Volume of mineral production . . . . 90% of 1928

Volume of factory employment . . . . 84% of 1928

Total of bank deposits . . . . 105% of 1928

Wholesale prices—all commodities . . . . 83% of 1928

Cost of living . . . . 94% of 1928

Various other indexes indicate total decrease of activity from 1928 of from 15 to 20 per cent.

There are many factors which give encouragement for the future. The fact that we are holding from 80 to 85 per cent of our normal activities and incomes; that our major financial and industrial institutions have come through the storm unimpaired; that price levels of major commodities have remained approximately stable for some time; that a number of industries are showing signs of increasing demand; that the world at large is readjusting itself to the situation; all reflect grounds for confidence. We should remember that these occasions have been met many times before, that they are but temporary, that our country is today stronger and richer in resources, in equipment, in skill, than ever in its history. We are in an extraordinary degree self-sustaining, we will overcome world influences and will lead the march of prosperity as we have always done hitherto.

Economic depression can not be cured by legislative action or executive pronouncement. Economic wounds must be healed by the action of the cells of the economic body—the producers and consumers themselves. Recovery can be expedited and its effects mitigated by cooperative action. That cooperation requires that every individual should sustain faith and courage; that each should maintain his self-reliance; that each and every one should search for methods of improving his business or service; that the vast majority whose income is unimpaired should not hoard out of fear but should pursue their normal living and recreations; that each should seek to assist his neighbors who may be less fortunate; that each industry should assist its own employees; that each community and each state should assume its full responsibilities for organization of employment and relief of distress with that sturdiness and independence which built a great Nation.

Our people are responding to these impulses in remarkable degree.

The best contribution of government lies in encouragement of this voluntary cooperation in the community. The Government, National, state, and local, can join with the community in such programs and do its part. A year ago I, together with other officers of the Government, initiated extensive cooperative measures throughout the country.

The first of these measures was an agreement of leading employers to maintain the standards of wages and of labor leaders to use their influence against strife. In a large sense these undertakings have been adhered to and we have not witnessed the usual reductions of wages which have always heretofore marked depressions. The index of union wage scales shows them to be today fully up to the level of any of the previous three years. In consequence the buying power of the country has been much larger than would otherwise have been the case. Of equal importance the Nation has had unusual peace in industry and freedom from the public disorder which has characterized previous depressions.

The second direction of cooperation has been that our governments, National, state, and local, the industries and business so distribute employment as to give work to the maximum number of employees.

The third direction of cooperation has been to maintain and even extend construction work and betterments in anticipation of the future. It has been the universal experience in previous depressions that public works and private construction have fallen off rapidly with the general tide of depression. On this occasion, however, the increased authorization and generous appropriations by the Congress and the action of states and municipalities have resulted in the expansion of public construction to an amount even above that in the most prosperous years. In addition the cooperation of public utilities, railways, and other large organizations has been generously given in construction and betterment work in anticipation of future need. The Department of Commerce advises me that as a result, the volume of this type of construction work, which amounted to roughly $6,300,000,000 in 1929, instead of decreasing will show a total of about $7,000,000,000 for 1930. There has, of course, been a substantial decrease in the types of construction which could not be undertaken in advance of need.

The fourth direction of cooperation was the organization in such states and municipalities, as was deemed necessary, of committees to organize local employment, to provide for employment agencies, and to effect relief of distress.

The result of magnificent cooperation throughout the country has been that actual suffering has been kept to a minimum during the past 12 months, and our unemployment has been far less in proportion than in other large industrial countries. Some time ago it became evident that unemployment would continue over the winter and would necessarily be added to from seasonal causes and that the savings of work-people would be more largely depleted. We have as a nation a definite duty to see that no deserving person in our country suffers from hunger or cold. I therefore set up a more extensive organization to stimulate more intensive cooperation throughout the country. There has been a most gratifying degree of response, from governors, mayors, and other public officials, from welfare organizations, and from employers in concerns both large and small. The local communities through their voluntary agencies have assumed the duty of relieving individual distress and are being generously supported by the public.

The number of those wholly out of employment seeking for work was accurately determined by the census last April as about 2,500,000. The Department of Labor index of employment in the larger trades shows some decrease in employment since that time. The problem from a relief point of view is somewhat less than the published estimates of the number of unemployed would indicate. The intensive community and individual efforts in providing special employment outside the listed industries are not reflected in the statistical indexes and tend to reduce such published figures. Moreover, there is estimated to be a constant figure at all times of nearly 1,000,000 unemployed who are not without annual income but temporarily idle in the shift from one job to another. We have an average of about three breadwinners to each two families, so that every person unemployed does not represent a family without income. The view that the relief problems are less than the gross numbers would indicate is confirmed by the experience of several cities, which shows that the number of families in distress represents from 10 to 20 per cent of the number of the calculated unemployed. This is not said to minimize the very real problem which exists but to weigh its actual proportions.

As a contribution to the situation the Federal Government is engaged upon the greatest program of waterway, harbor, flood control, public building, highway, and airway improvement in all our history. This, together with loans to merchant shipbuilders, improvement of the Navy and in military aviation, and other construction work of the Government will exceed $520,000,000 for this fiscal year. This compares with $253,000,000 in the fiscal year 1928. The construction works already authorized and the continuation of policies in Government aid will require a continual expenditure upwards of half a billion dollars annually.

I favor still further temporary expansion of these activities in aid to unemployment during this winter. The Congress will, however, have presented to it numbers of projects, some of them under the guise of, rather than the reality of, their usefulness in the increase of employment during the depression. There are certain common-sense limitations upon any expansions of construction work. The Government must not undertake works that are not of sound economic purpose and that have not been subject to searching technical investigation, and which have not been given adequate consideration by the Congress. The volume of construction work in the Government is already at the maximum limit warranted by financial prudence as a continuing policy. To increase taxation for purposes of construction work defeats its own purpose, as such taxes directly diminish employment in private industry. Again any kind of construction requires, after its authorization, a considerable time before labor can be employed in which to make engineering, architectural, and legal preparations. Our immediate problem is the increase of employment for the next six months, and new plans which do not produce such immediate result or which extend commitments beyond this period are not warranted.

The enlarged rivers and harbors, public building, and highway plans authorized by the Congress last session, however, offer an opportunity for assistance by the temporary acceleration of construction of these programs even faster than originally planned, especially if the technical requirements of the laws which entail great delays could be amended in such fashion as to speed up acquirements of land and the letting of contracts.

With view, however, to the possible need for acceleration, we, immediately upon receiving those authorities from the Congress five months ago, began the necessary technical work in preparation for such possible eventuality. I have canvassed the departments of the Government as to the maximum amount that can be properly added to our present expenditure to accelerate all construction during the next six months, and I feel warranted in asking the Congress for an appropriation of from $100,000,000 to $150,000,000 to provide such further employment in this emergency. In connection therewith we need some authority to make enlarged temporary advances of Federal-highway aid to the states.

I recommend that this appropriation be made distributable to the different departments upon recommendation of a committee of the Cabinet and approval by the President. Its application to works already authorized by the Congress assures its use in directions of economic importance and to public welfare. Such action will imply an expenditure upon construction of all kinds of over $650,000,000 during the next twelve months.

The world-wide depression has affected agriculture in common with all other industries. The average price of farm produce has fallen to about 80 per cent of the levels of 1928. This average is, however, greatly affected by wheat and cotton, which have participated in world-wide overproduction and have fallen to about 60 per cent of the average price of the year 1928. Excluding these commodities, the prices of all other agricultural products are about 84 per cent of those of 1928. The average wholesale prices of other primary goods, such as nonferrous metals, have fallen to 76 per cent of 1928.

The price levels of our major agricultural commodities are, in fact, higher than those in other principal producing countries, due to the combined result of the tariff and the operations of the Farm Board. For instance, wheat prices at Minneapolis are about 30 per cent higher than at Winnipeg, and at Chicago they are about 20 per cent higher than at Buenos Aires. Corn prices at Chicago are over twice as high as at Buenos Aires. Wool prices average more than 80 per cent higher in this country than abroad, and butter is 30 per cent higher in New York City than in Copenhagen.

Aside from the misfortune to agriculture of the world-wide depression we have had the most severe drought. It has affected particularly the states bordering on the Potomac, Ohio, and Lower Mississippi Rivers, with some areas in Montana, Kansas, Oklahoma, and Texas. It has found its major expression in the shortage of pasturage and a shrinkage in the corn crop from an average of about 2,800,000,000 bushels to about 2,090,000,000 bushels.

On August 14, I called a conference of the governors of the most acutely affected states, and as a result of its conclusions I appointed a national committee comprising the heads of the important Federal agencies under the chairmanship of the Secretary of Agriculture. The governors in turn have appointed state committees representative of the farmers, bankers, business men, and the Red Cross, and subsidiary committees have been established in most of the acutely affected counties. Railway rates were reduced on feed and livestock in and out of the drought areas, and over 50,000 cars of such products have been transported under these reduced rates. The Red Cross established a preliminary fund of $5,000,000 for distress relief purposes and established agencies for its administration in each county. Of this fund less than $500,000 has been called for up to this time as the need will appear more largely during the winter. The Federal Farm Loan Board has extended its credit facilities, and the Federal Farm Board has given financial assistance to all affected cooperatives.

In order that the Government may meet its full obligation toward our countrymen in distress through no fault of their own, I recommend that an appropriation should be made to the Department of Agriculture to be loaned for the purpose of seed and feed for animals. Its application should as hitherto in such loans be limited to a gross amount to any one individual, and secured upon the crop.

The Red Cross can relieve the cases of individual distress by the sympathetic assistance of our people. . . .

HERBERT HOOVER

The White House,
December 2, 1930

8

Message
to the
Press: 1931

On February 3, 1931, Hoover spoke to the press of his willingness to employ unprecedented powers in order to alleviate distress, and reviewed his actions in this regard. At the same time, the message indicated he still did not grasp fully the seriousness of the depression.

Document†
Certain senators have issued a public statement to the effect that unless the President and the House of Representatives agree to appropriations from the Federal Treasury for charitable purposes they will force an extra session of Congress.

I do not wish to add acrimony to a discussion, but would rather state this case as I see its fundamentals.

This is not an issue as to whether people shall go hungry or cold in the United States. It is solely a question of the best method by which hunger and cold shall be prevented. It is a question as to whether the American people, on one hand, will maintain the spirit of charity and mutual self-help through voluntary giving and the responsibility of local government as distinguished, on the other hand, from appropriations out of the Federal Treasury for such purposes. My own conviction is strongly that if we break down this sense of responsibility of individual generosity to individual and mutual self-help in the country in times of national difficulty and if we start appropriations of this character we have not only impaired something infinitely valuable in the life of the American people but have struck at the roots of self-government. . . .

And there is a practical problem in all this. The help being daily extended by neighbors, by local and national agencies, by municipalities, by industry and a great multitude of organizations throughout the country today is many times any appropriation yet proposed. The opening of the doors of the Federal Treasury is likely to stifle this giving and thus destroy far more resources than the proposed charity from the Federal Government.

The basis of successful relief in national distress is to mobilize and organize the infinite number of agencies of self-help in the community. That has been the American way of relieving distress among our own people, and the country is successfully meeting its problem in the American way today.

†From: Myers, *State Papers*, vol. I, p. 496. Reprinted by permission of the Herbert Hoover Foundation.

We have two entirely separate and distinct situations in the country; the first is the drought area; the second is the unemployment in our large industrial centers—for both of which these appopriations attempt to make charitable contributions.

Immediately upon the appearance of the drought last August, I convoked a meeting of the governors, the Red Cross and the railways, the bankers and other agencies in the country and laid the foundations of organization and the resources . . . to meet the situation. . . .

The organization has stretched throughout the area of suffering, the people are being cared for . . . no one is going hungry and no one need go hungry or cold.

To reinforce this work at the opening of Congress I recommend large appropriations for loans to rehabilitate agriculture from the drought and provision of further large sums for public works and construction in the drought territory, which would give employment in further relief to the whole situation. . . .

In the matter of unemployment outside of the drought areas, important economic measures of mutual self-help have been developed such as those to maintain wages, to distribute employment equitably, to increase construction work by industry, to increase Federal construction work from a rate of about $275,000,000 a year prior to the depression to a rate now of over $750,000,000 a year; to expand State and municipal construction—all upon a scale never before provided or even attempted in any depression. But beyond this to assure that there shall be no suffering, in every town and county voluntary agencies in relief of distress have been strengthened and created and generous funds have been placed at their disposal. They are carrying on their work efficiently and sympathetically.

But after and coincidently with voluntary relief our American system requires that municipal, county, and State governments shall use their own resources and credit before seeking such assistance from the Federal Treasury.

I have indeed spent much of my life in fighting hardship and starvation both abroad and in the Southern States. I do not feel that I should be charged with lack of human sympathy for those who suffer, but I recall that in all the organizations with which I have been connected over these many years, the foundation has been to summon the maximum of self-help. I am proud to have sought the help of Congress in the past for nations who were so disorganized by war and anarchy that self-help was impossible. But even these appropriations were but a tithe of that which was coincidently mobilized from the public charity of the United States and foreign countries. There is no such paralysis in the United States and I am confident that our people have the resources, the initiative, the courage, the stamina and kindliness of spirit to meet this situation in the way they have met their problems over generations.

. . . *I am willing to pledge myself* that if the time should ever come that the voluntary agencies of the country together with the local and State governments are unable to find resources with which to prevent hunger and suffering in my country, *I will ask the aid of every resource of the Federal Government because I would no more see starvation amongst our countrymen than would any senator or congressman.* I have faith in the American people that such a day will not come.

The American people are doing their job today. . . .

The whole business situation would be greatly strengthened by the prompt completion of the necessary legislation of this session of Congress and thereby the unemployment problem would be lessened. . . .

9

Words of Criticism

Washington reporter Robert Allen in 1931 took a dim view of the Hoover efforts, calling them more talk than action. In particular, Allen was critical of Hoover's support of the Smoot-Hawley Tariff. The Allen view soon became the "accepted truth" as to Hoover's actions during the first year of the depression.

Document†

In the long and tragic travail of the economic depression, the most tragic thing was the President's fear of admitting that a great disaster had befallen the country. For months, while gloom, unemployment, and deflation settled on the land, he refused to admit their reality or do anything fundamental about the situation. His approach to the problem was wholly that of the boomer, the bull-marker operator, concerned only with his own political interests and willing to resort to any device or misrepresentation to further them.

Facts, statistics, plan, organization—there have been none, and when proposed by others have been rejected and stifled, secretly when possible, openly when that was impossible.

One policy alone has dominated his course: not to do or say anything that would reveal the truth about the great catastrophe. Suppression and inaction have been his unshaken rule.

The detailed record of this effort tells the story eloquently:

On December 14, 1929, Mr. Hoover declared that the volume of shopping reported to him indicated that the business of the country was "back to normal." That was some six weeks after the stock market crash.

Early in January, 1930, Secretary of the Treasury Mellon, under pressure from Hoover, announced, "I see nothing in the present situation that is either menacing or warrants pessimism. I have every confidence that there will be a revival of activity in the spring." These ebullient assurances were greeted with a drop in stock market prices to new low levels.

A year and five months later Mr. Mellon, addressing a group of international bankers in Washington, and apparently free for the moment from White House restraint, frankly admitted: "I have no means of knowing when or how we shall emerge from the valley in which we are now traveling."

On January 22, the President personally expressed the view that the

†From: Robert A. Allen and Drew Pearson, *Washington Merry-Go-Round* (New York: H. Liveright, Inc., 1931), pp. 74-77. Reprinted by permission of the estate of Drew Pearson.

"trend" of employment had changed upward and then Secretary of Labor Davis, carrying out the refrain, gave it on his word that "every major industry was showing increases and that we can expect a great deal of business in 1930."

In February and early March, Secretary of Commerce Lamont, acting on White House orders, took up the burden and on three occasions solemnly gave assurance that "there is nothing in the situation to be disturbed about."

All this time, according to the most reliable labor statistics available in the United States at present, those of the New York State Labor Bureau, factories were closing down in increasing numbers and the unemployment line was steadily lengthening.

On March 8, 1930, the President himself again entered the lists with his now famous prediction that the crisis would be over in "sixty days." (See May 2 statement below.)

On March 16, Julius H. Barnes, close personal friend and under-cover agent for the President, as Chairman of the President's National Business Survey Conference, declared "that the spring of 1930 marks the end of a period of grave concern." Barnes failed to add however that others would follow of even greater gravity.

On May 2, the President, with the expiration of his "sixty days," trimmed his sails very sharply. In a lengthy pronouncement he conceded that things were rather disturbed, but was still irrepressibly optimistic. "We have been passing through one of those great economic storms which periodically bring hardships and suffering to our people," he admitted. "While the crisis took place only six months ago, I am convinced we have passed the worst and with continued unity of effort we shall rapidly recover."

Two months later, in the privacy of his office and under strict and repeated admonitions of secrecy, he petulantly told Amos Pinchot and a group of important business men who had called to urge him to do something drastic to relieve unemployment: "Gentlemen, you are six weeks too late. The crisis is over."

Three months later, with bread lines longer than ever before and facing state and congressional elections, he set up, amid much fanfare, a national unemployment committee to "coördinate" employment activities.

In January, 1931, Colonel Arthur Woods, director of the committee, summoned before a Senate committee to tell about his work, estimated unemployment as around 5,000,000 and informed the Senators that his organization was preparing to disseminate pamphlets on how to stimulate relief. A week later the President issued a proclamation asking the public to contribute $10,000,000 to the Red Cross for food relief.

Three months later the Census Bureau announced that a special unemployment survey it had made showed an estimated 6,050,000 out of work.

The President's actions leading up to his signing the Smoot-Hawley Tariff Act probably were the most vacillating of his entire career. Three days before he announced he would approve it, one of his secretaries categorically informed reporters that the President had not made up his mind about the measure and would make no decision until it had come to him from Congress and he had sent it to the various departments and received their formal views on the matter.

This story was printed far and wide. Seventy-two hours later, while the Act was still unfinished legislation in Congress, the President let it be known that he would approve it. The reasons he gave for bowing before a tariff act, every one knew he bitterly resented, were thus characterized by Senator Pat Harrison on the floor of the Senate:

"This statement is unworthy of the President. It is one of the most intellectually dishonest statements ever to come from the White House."

10

Criticism from the Press

What was the alternative? Columnist Walter Lippmann, a Wilsonian progressive, mildly rebuked Hoover for his actions, but had little more to offer by way of change than a balanced budget. In effect, he chastised Hoover for being too much of a spender in an article published on December 16, 1931.

Document†
The A B C of the deficit; balancing the Federal accounts the central problem in combating the depression.

For the first time within the experience of most of us the United States government has a serious financial problem. Most Americans are accustomed to the comfortable belief that the Federal power is inexhaustibly rich. It financed the great war lavishly. In the post-war decade it was able for many years to reduce taxes and yet accumulate fat surpluses. It is hard for the country to realize that this era of easy finance is over, and that we are left today with greatly diminished incomes, greatly increased current expenditures, and most of the war still to be paid for. In respect to government finance, as in respect to so many other things, Congress and the people of the country have radically to readjust their minds.

It is well to get the fundamental figures clearly fixed in our minds, and for that purpose round numbers are all that it is necessary to remember. Let us see then what the Federal government is spending this year, remembering that when we speak of the government's financial year we mean the twelve months from July 1, 1931, to June 30, 1932.

We are spending 4,500 million dollars. On what? 1,000 millions goes to pay interest and principal on the debt. It is chiefly the cost of the last war. Nearly another 1,000 millions goes to the veterans of former wars. A little over 700 millions goes to the army and navy. This accounts for half of our expenditures.

The actual running of the government, of Congress, the courts, the executive departments, commissions, bureaus, and civil pensions cost a little more than 400 millions. This includes a postal deficit of 156 millions.

On various kinds of public services, public works and subsidies we are spending another 1,000 million. This includes small expenditures on such

†From: Walter Lippmann, *Interpretations, 1931-1932* (New York, 1932), pp. 57-60. Reprinted with permission of Macmillan Publishing Co., Inc., from Interpretations: 1931-32, by Walter Lippmann. Copyright 1932 by Walter Lippmann, renewed 1960 by Allan Nevins.

things as education and public health, huge expenditures of more than 200 millions to help agriculture, of nearly 150 millions to help the merchant marine, and of more than 500 millions on public buildings and public works.

Finally we are spending about 250 millions on miscellaneous items such as refunds, administering the District of Columbia, and so forth.

The figures may be put in another way in order to remember them. The cost of running the executive, legislative and judicial branches of the government is one-tenth of the total expenditures. Of the remaining 4,000 millions about one-quarter goes to the debt, one-quarter goes to the veterans, one-quarter goes to public works and subsidies, three-sixteenths to the army and navy, and one-sixteenth to sundries.

Let us look now at the revenues for this year. We have only estimates, for the year is only half over, and it is not possible to predict exactly what can be collected in the remaining six months. But the Treasury estimate is that the government will receive about 2,360 millions. This is just about enough to pay for the debt, the veterans, and the navy. For the army, the whole cost of the government, and all the public works and subsidies, there are no revenues. They have to be paid for by borrowing. If we regard the debt, the veterans, and the navy as our first fixed national charges, then it may be said that the Federal government's revenues this year will just meet their fixed charges, and for everything else it is compelled to borrow.

The next thing to fix in mind is the immediate reason for this financial position. It can be put most clearly in this way: since the last full year of prosperity, which was the year ending June 30, 1929, the government's expenditures have *increased* more than 16 per cent and its revenues have *decreased* more than 40 per cent. The increased expenditure during the Hoover Administration is not fairly measured by this 16 per cent. For the dollar in terms of purchasing power is worth about 10 per cent more, which means that the expenditures this year, measured in purchasing power, are about 25 per cent heavier than at the beginning of this Administration.

To meet this increasing weight of expenditure we have a tax system which is peculiarly vulnerable to a depression. Being based largely on incomes and capital gains and on customs, it has no stability in a depression. The Under Secretary of the Treasury, Mr. Mills, said on Monday night, that whereas the government collected 1,000 millions from corporations in 1930 it will collect only half that much this year. When the figures for income tax this year become really available, it will be shown that it is a deeply unsatisfactory basis of revenue as it is now arranged.

The people of this country face in really serious and practical form the problem of reducing the cost of government and of increasing the revenues of government. All other projects revolve about this central question of how to balance the Federal accounts.

Part three

Bibliographic Essay

There is no satisfactory biography of Herbert Hoover. This is so, less from lack of interest in the subject, than from the fact that until recently, many of the papers and records of his administration have been closed to scholars. Even now, materials dealing with Hoover's business and engineering careers are sealed.

Historians are busily mining the newly-released records, and we may expect significant Hoover books, monographs, and articles to be released in the mid- and late 1970s. Present indications are that these will be sympathetic, and probably well-received. There is a revived interest in Hoover, most particularly on the part of the New Left historians. There is some irony in this, for Hoover was repelled by many of their assumptions regarding the nature of American life. But for reasons different from those of the New Left, he railed against strong government, was concerned with individual rights vis-à-vis those of the government, and many of his statements can be interpreted as isolationist. In the past, Hoover was condemned for things he did not do, statements he did not utter. Now, after having been castigated for the wrong reasons for so long, he may be praised for them.

Until records are released, the most complete biography remains Eugene Lyons, *Herbert Hoover: A Biography* (Garden City, 1964). Earlier Lyons wrote *Our Unknown Ex-President: A Portrait of Herbert Hoover* (Garden City, 1948). Neither book shows much depth of research or critical facilities on the part of the author. Instead, they are two of a string of books, published from 1933 to the present by conservatives, that attempt to defend Hoover and free enterprise against attacks by New Dealers and liberals. In the process, Lyons seems more interested with what Hoover said than what he did. Finally, he helped create the myth now being adopted by the New Left. A far more perceptive work is William Hard, *Who's Hoover?* (New York, 1928). Although he wrote prior to the 1928 presidential election, and did so with no documentation and little research, Hard offers a sensitive and perceptive analysis of Hoover's character, noting strong and weak points alike. No one who had read and digested Hard's book should have been surprised by Hoover's actions as president and, later on, public citizen. Other pro-Hoover works of this period are Will Irwin, *Herbert Hoover: A Reminiscent Biography* (New York, 1928), Samuel Crowther, *The Presidency Vs. Hoover* (Garden City, 1928), and Edwin Emerson, *Hoover and His Times: Looking Back Through the Years* (Garden City, 1932). Also, see William J. Marsh, *Our President, Herbert Hoover* (New Milford, Conn., 1930) for a most adulatory work and David Hinshaw, *Herbert Hoover, American Quaker* (New York, 1950) for an attempt to interprete almost all of Hoover's actions in the light of his Quaker heritage.

Hoover wrote widely of his career and beliefs. Indeed, no other president has attempted to justify and explain his actions as much as Hoover did in the 1930s and 1940s. For his own memories of his childhood, see *A Boyhood in Iowa* (New York, 1931). A picture of Hoover's humor, and the man at relaxation, can be found in *Fishing for Fun—And to Wash Your Soul* (New York, 1963). The World War I years are covered in *An American Epic*, 4 vols. (Garden City, 1959-1960), while Hoover's biography, *The Ordeal of Woodrow Wilson* (New York, 1958), deals more with his relationship with the wartime president than anything else. *American Individualism* (Garden City, 1922) is a short and clear statement of Hoover's philosophy and beliefs regarding the American people. *The New Day: Campaign Speeches of Herbert Hoover, 1928* (Stanford, 1928) is an excellent collection. *Addresses Upon the American Road, 1933-1938* (New York, 1938) contains several speeches in which Hoover defended his policies and attacked the Roosevelt alternatives. Five additional collections of Hoover's speeches were published under the same title, taking his activities up to 1960. Finally, Hoover's *Memoirs* 3 vols. (New York, 1951-1952) present his own view of his life and career. The work is marred by excessive defenses of policies and distortions, however.

William S. Myers, ed. *The State Papers and Other Public Writings of Herbert Hoover* 2 vols. (Garden City, 1934) is the handiest collection of the official record. In collaboration with Walter H. Newton, Myers wrote and edited *The Hoover Administration: A Documented Narrative* (New York, 1936), a biased but accurate day-by-day record of the administration's activities. This work contains portions of Hoover's speeches, as well as the words of his defenders and critics. Theodore G. Joslin, *Hoover Off the Record* (Garden City, 1935), is written by a former Hoover secretary who admired the president greatly. Ray L. Wilbur and Arthur M. Hyde, *The Hoover Policies* (New York, 1937), is a collection of his statements and writings, set down in topical manner and tied together by a narrative.

Special aspects of Hoover's career have been the subject of monographs in recent years. Joseph Brandes, *Herbert Hoover and Economic Diplomacy: Department of Commerce Policy, 1921-1928* (Pittsburgh, 1962), is far broader than its title indicates and a key work in the field. Harris G. Warren, *Herbert Hoover and the Great Depression* (New York, 1959) is a useful work drawn almost entirely from previously published works and newspaper and magazine articles and reports. Albert U. Romasco, *The Poverty of Abundance: Hoover, the Nation, the Depression* (New York, 1965) is perceptive though somewhat dull. Walter F. Dexter, *Herbert Hoover and American Individualism: A Modern Interpretation of a National Ideal* (New York, 1932) is overly defensive and shrill, as were most of the pro-Hoover biographies of that period.

The associational movement is well covered in James W. Prothro, *The Dollar Decade: Business Ideas in the 1920's* (Baton Rouge, 1954). For an appreciation of the origins of associationalism, see E.H. Naylor, *Trade Associations* (New York, 1921); Forrest Crissey, *Teamwork in Trade-Building* (New York, 1914); Edward Hurley, *Awakening of Business* (New York, 1917); Arthur Eddy, *The New Competition* (New York, 1912); and E.H. Gaunt, *Co-operative Competition* (Providence, 1917). Louis Galambos, *Competition and Cooperation: The Emergence of a National Trade Association* (Baltimore, 1966), is the definitive work in the field. Norman W. Storer, *The Social System of Science* (New York, 1966); Horace M. Drury, *Scientific Management*, 3rd ed. (New York, 1922); and Samuel Haber, *Efficiency and Uplift: Scientific Management in the Progressive Era, 1890-1920* (Chicago, 1964), indicate Hoover's relationship with the movement, and the links between science and technology on the one hand and business organization on the other. Herbert Hoover, "The Scientists' and Engineers' Promise to American Life," *Centennial of Engineering, 1852-1952* (New York, 1953), is disappointing, however. Also see Robert H. Wiebe, *Businessmen and Reform: A Study of the Progressive Movement* (Cambridge, 1962), Robert G. McCloskey, *American Conservatism in the Age of Enterprise, 1865-1910* (Cambridge, 1951), and Thomas C. Cochran, *American Business in the Twentieth Century* (Cambridge, 1972) for background. William E. Leuchtenburg, *The Perils of Prosperity, 1914-1932* (Chicago, 1958) is a fine study of the inter-war period. John D. Hicks, *Republican Ascendancy, 1921-1933* (New York, 1960) is more complete but less original. Karl Shriftgiesser, *This Was Normalcy* (Boston, 1948) and Dixon Wecter, *The Age of the Great Depression, 1929-1941* (New York, 1948) are readable anti-Hoover works. Arthur M. Schlesinger, Jr., *The Age of Roosevelt: The Crisis of the Old Order, 1919-1933* (Boston, 1957) is better balanced though also partisan. Gene Smith, *The Shattered Dream: Herbert Hoover and the Great Depression* (New York, 1970) is a work of sensitivity that did much to revive interest in Hoover among the general population.

The depression and its origins have been the subjects of many books and articles, none of which has satisfactorally analyzed its causes. The most famous of these is John K. Galbraith, *The Great Crash* (Boston, 1954), which is generally anti-business and anti-Republican. Galbraith blames the crash on excesses on Wall Street and myopia in business and government. Robert Sobel, *The Great Bull Market: Wall Street in the 1920s* (New York, 1968) is an attempt at a corrective, which holds that the stock market crash was not as severe as most believe it to have been today. Lionel Robbins, *The Great Depression* (London, 1934) is an early view of the depression written by an Englishman. Richard T. Ely, *Hard Times—The Way In and the Way Out* (New York, 1932) is by an American economist of that period.

In order to understand alternatives to the Hoover program one should read the contemporary books and articles by his critics. See Edmund Wilson, *The American Jitters: A Year of the Slump* (New York, 1932); Walter Lippman, *Interpretations, 1931-1932);* Lawrence Dennis, *Is Capitalism Doomed?* (New York, 1932); Felix Morley, ed., *Aspects of the Depression* (Chicago, 1932); Samuel Crowther, ed., *A Basis of Stability* (Boston, 1932); and Gilbert Seldes, *The Years of the Locust, America, 1929-1932* (Boston, 1933).

The "conventional wisdom" regarding meeting the depression may be found in several government publications. United States, *Report of the President's Conference on Unemployment, September 26 to October 13, 1921* (Washington, 1921) and United States, Conference on Unemployment, Committee on Unemployment and Business Cycles, *Business Cycles and Unemployment* (New York, 1923) are particularly worthwhile. United States, President's Conference on Unemployment, *Recent Economic Changes in the United States*. 2 vols. (New York, 1929) is vital for an understanding of the Hoover approach. In it Hoover and others indicate what their brand of activism will be in case of a depression—like the one that came less than a year after the conference adjourned. Edward E. Hunt, *An Audit of America* (New York, 1930) is a summary and analysis of *Recent Economic Changes*.

It would be impractical to even attempt to list and analyze significant articles published in 1929 and the early 1930s regarding Hoover and the depression. Literally dozens of journals devoted the bulk of their space to the subject. The best of these were *Forum, Survey, North American Review, Review of Reviews, World's Work, Saturday Evening Post, Atlantic, Harper's, Nation, New Republic, Current History,* and *Time* are of particular interest. Several issues of *Annals of the American Academy of Political and Social Science* were devoted to depression-related issues. In particular see, that of March, 1931 (vol. 154) to see how the nation's "best minds" viewed the decline at the end of its first year.

Finally, two works should be carefully read by all serious students of the subject. Jordan A. Schwarz, *The Interregnum of Despair: Hoover, Congress, and the Depression* (Urbana, 1970) is well-balanced and written, and easily the best of the recent monographs in the area. Arnold S. Rice, ed. *Herbert Hoover, 1874-1964: Chronology-Documents-Bibliographical Aids* (Dobbs Ferry, 1971) contains unimaginative documents and an inadequate bibliography, but the chronology section is of great use for Hoover scholars in that it has been carefully gathered and is accurate.